WITH KINDEST REGARDS

À Charles L. Freer — à un de ces jours.

1909

WITH KINDEST REGARDS

THE CORRESPONDENCE OF

Charles Lang Freer

AND

James McNeill Whistler

1890–1903

Edited by Linda Merrill

Freer Gallery of Art, Smithsonian Institution, Washington, D.C.
Smithsonian Institution Press, Washington, D.C., and London

Published by the Freer Gallery of Art, Smithsonian
Institution, Washington, D.C., and Smithsonian
Institution Press, Washington and London.

Edited by Mary Kay Zuravleff
Designed by Carol Beehler
Typeset in Adobe Garamond
Printed and bound in Canada

Library of Congress Cataloging-in-Publication Data
Freer, Charles Lang, 1854–1919.
With kindest regards: the correspondence of Charles
Lang Freer and James McNeill Whistler, 1890–1903 /
edited by Linda Merrill.
p. cm.
Includes bibliographical references and index.
ISBN 1-56098-532-1 (alk. paper)
1. Freer, Charles Lang, 1854–1919—Correspondence.
2. Art patrons—United States—Correspondence.
3. Whistler, James McNeill, 1834–1903. I. Whistler,
James McNeill, 1834–1903. II. Merrill, Linda, 1959–
III. Title.
N5220.F64A4   1995
709'.2—dc20
[B]   94-48202
                                             CIP

The paper used in this publication meets the minimum
requirements for the American National Standard for
Permanence of Paper for Printed Library Materials,
Z39.49–1984.

Photographic Credits
Unless otherwise indicated, vintage photographs and
primary source materials are in the Charles Lang Freer
Papers, Freer Gallery Archives. All works illustrated
are in the collection of the Freer Gallery of Art.
Frontispiece: James McNeill Whistler, 1885.
Photogravure attributed to Mortimer Menpes
(1859–1938). Signed with the butterfly and inscribed
by Whistler, probably in 1899, "To Charles L. Freer—
à un de ces jours!"

Contents

Foreword
Milo Cleveland Beach
6

Preface
8

Introduction: Tokens of Esteem
13

Color Plates
49

Letters
65

Appendix A. "A Day with Whistler," from the
Detroit Free Press
194

Appendix B. Prints Listed in the Correspondence
199

Bibliography
209

Index
211

FOREWORD

*T*he friendship that developed between Charles Lang Freer, the American businessman and collector, and the artist James McNeill Whistler had unusually fruitful repercussions. Freer had begun a modest collection of paintings, drawings, and prints (including works by Whistler) when he first met the artist in 1890; at the time of Freer's death in 1919, however, his Whistler collection was the largest in the world. Among interests that brought the two men together was Japanese art. Whistler's belief that the Japanese works available in Europe were only the "last gasp" of an ancient tradition certainly played a role in Freer's decision to visit Asia. During the five trips he made between 1894 and 1911, Freer acquired many of the great works of Asian art that have joined his Whistler collection at the Freer Gallery of Art in Washington, D.C.

The relationship between Freer and Whistler has been discussed in a recent publication, *Freer: A Legacy of Art,* written by Linda Merrill and Thomas Lawton. In this volume, Dr. Merrill has assembled and commented on the surviving correspondence between the two men. The book presents eighty-nine documents (letters, cablegrams, telegrams, and calling cards) spanning 1890 through 1903. The first is Freer's letter thanking Whistler and his wife for their hospitality on the occasion of their first meeting in Whistler's London studio; the last is Whistler's request for a visit from Freer, sent by telegram two days before Whistler died. The closing used in many of these letters, "with kindest regards," serves as the title of this work and also provides a cogent summation of the writers' mutual esteem.

The letters from Whistler are drawn from the Charles Lang Freer Papers in the archives of the Freer Gallery of Art, while the letters Freer wrote are housed in the Glasgow University Library. Together these two institutions are devoted to furthering research into Whistler's life and work. In addition to documenting the growth of Freer's collection, the letters also reveal the sincere friendship between the two men. Whistler found in Freer his most important patron, the man who would firmly establish his reputation in the United States. Freer, in turn, was honored by the company of an important artist and by Whistler's advice and help in shaping his collections. Although Whistler was notorious for his irascible nature, the letters to and from Freer reveal a genuineness and generosity that have largely gone unobserved.

The Whistler collection at the Freer Gallery includes 130 paintings, 174 drawings, and 946 prints, and the archival materials range from press clippings and photographs to records of virtually every piece of Whistler's work that Freer purchased. The presence of the artist is felt throughout the museum, even though now it principally houses a collection of Asian art. Without the support and enthusiasm of James McNeill Whistler, Freer's collection would have had a vastly different character. In fact, were it not for their friendship, Freer might never have dreamed of endowing a museum to preserve his collection and share it with the world.

MILO CLEVELAND BEACH, *Director*
Arthur M. Sackler Gallery and Freer Gallery of Art

PREFACE

The air of controversy that surrounded James McNeill Whistler during his life survived to influence his biography. *The Life of James McNeill Whistler,* first published in 1908, was written by Elizabeth and Joseph Pennell without the cooperation of Rosalind Birnie Philip, Whistler's heir and the executor of his estate. Because she did not believe Whistler had authorized the Pennells to undertake the project, she refused them access to the works and personal papers in her possession. Charles Lang Freer took her side in the dispute. As a result, he was effectively written out of Whistler's life.

In the Pennells' version of events, Freer became a peripheral figure, usually referred to anonymously as a rich American or, if by name, as owner of one or another of Whistler's works, as though his association with the artist had been purely financial. The biographers do acknowledge that Freer attended Whistler during two critical periods at the end of his life, yet in his single extended appearance in the book he is made the object of derision: describing a dinner at the Café Royal in 1899, the Pennells say that Freer entertained the party "by talking pictures, like a 'new critic,' and Japanese prints, like a cultured school-ma'am" while Whistler slept, awakening only to the sound of his own snores. The anecdote is unnecessarily cruel—the Pennells speak elsewhere of Whistler's habit of dozing after dinner—

and it seems likely that Freer was, as they say in *The Whistler Journal* of 1921, "mortally offended" by their recounting it. But they were mistaken in ascribing his enmity entirely to that offense, for Freer's opposition to their work, like other apparently unreasonable positions he assumed over the years, arose from his deeply rooted devotion to Whistler.

Subsequent biographies of the artist have also neglected the importance of Whistler's relationship with Freer. Even at the Freer Gallery of Art, the founder's intended tribute to Whistler has been obscured by the enormous growth in the Asian collections since Freer's bequest. The correspondence published here expands the story of Whistler's later years as it documents the development of Freer's collection. These missives reveal a friendship that was mutually beneficial yet sincere, and they hint of an unwritten agreement that inspired both Freer's gift to the nation and the strings he so securely attached to that gift. With his art collections, Freer bequeathed Whistler's letters to the Smithsonian Institution, where they remain in the Freer Gallery Archives. The earliest of these were written by the artist's wife, Beatrix Whistler, and some of the later letters were dictated by Whistler to Rosalind Philip. Freer was to maintain an active correspondence with Philip, and their letters might constitute another volume; a few of the first, exchanged in the last two years of Whistler's life, have been included in this edition. Rosalind Philip gave Freer's letters to the University of Glasgow in 1954, together with other personal papers from Whistler's estate. She had already presented a selection of her inherited paintings, drawings, and prints—stipulating, as Freer had, that they never leave the premises—and she bequeathed to the university the remainder of her Whistler collection. Housed in the Glasgow University Library, the papers are the nucleus of an extensive archive of primary documents and publications relating to Whistler's life and art. The works by Whistler in the university's Hunterian Art Gallery are rivaled only by those in the Freer Gallery of Art.

It is a special pleasure, therefore, to unite Whistler's and Freer's correspondence in a volume produced through the cooperation of those two institutions. The University of Glasgow granted permission to publish the letters, and Nigel Thorp, director of the university's Centre for Whistler Studies, sanctioned the project and helped it on its way. As the primary editor of Whistler's complete correspondence, in which these letters will eventually take their place, Dr. Thorp also provided inspiration through example.

I am pleased to acknowledge the Women's Committee of the Smithsonian Associates, which funded the conservation of *Nocturne: Blue and Silver—Bognor*, reproduced here for the first time in its revitalized state; and Wendy Hartman Samet, who wrought the miracle of conservation on the painting we had feared was lost. I also wish to thank John Siewert, who shared his careful transcriptions of the Whistler letters in the Freer Gallery Archives, and Mary Fletcher Jones, who helped produce initial typescripts of the Freer letters.

I am grateful to Thomas Lentz, assistant director for research and collections at the Freer and Sackler Galleries, for encouraging me to proceed with this publication and helping me to find the needed time; to John Tsantes and the staff of the photography department, for providing the reproductions that illustrate these pages; to Martha Smith, for helping me to survey the Whistler print collection; to Grace Liu, for cheerfully assisting with a wide variety of tasks; and to Lily Kecskes and Kathryn Phillips, for responding to countless queries in the library. Colleen Hennessey expertly organized the Charles Lang Freer Papers, greatly facilitating my research, and endured months of continual requests for documents and information with extraordinary grace and good will.

The book would not have been begun without Karen Sagstetter, editor in chief, who recognized its value and saw it through production. Carol Beehler, the designer, transformed a tangle of text into pages pleasurable to behold; and

Mary Kay Zuravleff, the editor, brought intellectual order to the manuscript and unstinting enthusiasm to its preparation. Working with these gifted colleagues has been an unqualified delight, and to them all I extend my kindest regards.

Following page: Charles Lang Freer comparing Whistler's *Venus Rising from the Sea* (03.174) to an Islamic ceramic pot (05.61), 1909. Photograph by Alvin Langdon Coburn (1882–1966).

Tokens of Esteem

$\mathcal{J}$ames McNeill Whistler (1834–1903) and Charles Lang Freer (1854–1919) were unlikely friends but ideal partners in a project accomplished through mutual regard. They met when Freer was a young industrialist, still cultivating a collection of prints, and Whistler was a well-known artist approaching the pinnacle of his career. The foundation of their friendship, which evolved over thirteen years, was their common conviction in Whistler's genius; its product was the unparalleled collection of his works preserved for posterity in the first national art museum of the United States. "Let it be frankly stated then," said Freer's friend and confidante Agnes Meyer, "that the Freer Gallery is above all things a tribute to the contemporary artist whom Mr. Freer most loved and admired, and to whom he owed, more than to any other single influence, his artistic bent and education."[1]

Freer paid his first call on Whistler in March 1890, intending to make a business proposition, not a friend. Since 1887, when fellow collector Howard Mansfield had introduced him to Whistler's etchings, Freer had searched the print shops of New York City, hoping to build a comparable collection of his own. Failing to find the quality he wanted at a price he could afford, Freer resolved to approach Whistler personally on his first trip to London; he hoped to arrange with Whistler to purchase choice impressions of each new print directly from the artist.[2] By removing the

Fig. 1. *Steps, Amsterdam* (K403), 1889. Etching, third state (24.1 x 16.4), 06.112.

dealer from the transaction, the plan he proposed would be, he thought, "mutually advantageous" (letter 2).

Belying the popular perception of his difficult personality, Whistler not only consented to the scheme but proved agreeable in every way: Freer later maintained that he would accommodate any stranger who accorded him "the formality and courtesy due a gentleman and an artist."[3] His own deference had been rewarded with a visit to Whistler's studio, where proofs of his latest prints had just come off the press (fig. 1). Etched in Amsterdam the previous year, the plates were so dense with detail that few impressions could be printed before the copper became irreparably worn, which made the ten proofs, specially selected and autographed by Whistler for Freer, collector's items of the highest order. Freer purchased a duplicate set for Mansfield, and each lent a few of his new possessions to a New York exhibition, where Whistler had predicted their success; his wife, Beatrix, had written from Holland to an American art dealer that the Amsterdam etchings were sure to be popular in New York City, coming as they did "from the country of the Knickerbockers."[4]

The etchings attracted attention in Detroit, as well, where Freer was beginning to make his fortune (fig. 2). He was thirty-six years old in 1890, vice president of a prospering company that manufactured railroad cars, and already in possession of a local reputation as a patron of the arts. At the Witenagemote, a private club dedicated to the increase of culture, Freer exhibited his set of Amsterdam etchings and presented an informal talk about his recent encounter with the artist. Afterward, he told his story to the *Detroit Free Press,* hoping to dispel some myths regarding Whistler's fractious nature. The resulting article (appendix A) failed to meet Freer's standards of accuracy, and when he sent a copy to Whistler he apologized for its "blunders" (letter 1). He may have regretted granting the interview at all, for he would never again speak publicly about his association with Whistler. Freer came to detest nothing more than the "silly vaporings" of people who used their acquaintance with "the master" to achieve a modicum of fame for themselves.[5]

Freer wanted only prints from Whistler. Having been assured that other works would follow the Amsterdam etchings to Detroit, Freer issued polite reminders to the artist that he was waiting across the Atlantic, hungry for something new. Occasionally, he would betray some annoyance at Whistler's apparent failure to uphold his end of their agreement;[6] but when he received a choice impression of the artist's first new etching in 1891, and packages replete with exquisitely printed lithographs in 1892 and 1894, he learned that with Whistler, it paid to be patient. Recognizing Freer's indulgence, Beatrix Whistler sketched him as a patron saint, encircling his head with a halo.[7]

Whistler's inattention to Freer's standing order for prints could be partly excused by his growing preoccupation, in the early 1890s, with the change in his fortunes. In 1891

Fig. 2. Charles Lang Freer, ca. 1890.

the Corporation of Glasgow purchased his portrait of Thomas Carlyle, *Arrangement in Grey and Black, No. 2,* and a few months later the French government bought *Arrangement in Grey and Black: Portrait of the Artist's Mother* (fig. 3) for its national museum of contemporary art, the Musée du Luxembourg. Although Whistler could not have imagined that the portrait of his mother was destined to become the most recognized American painting of the nineteenth century, he considered its acquisition by the French a solemn consecration.[8] He had long acknowledged the need to place his works in public collections, where they would never disappear from what he called "the story of the painter's reputation."[9]

As Beatrix Whistler informed Freer, the French commendation brought about a surprising change of tone in the London papers (letter 11). Ever alert to the opinions of the press, Whistler dedicated himself to organizing a retrospective that would amplify this English reevaluation. With David Croal Thomson, director of the Goupil Gallery in London, he oversaw every aspect of the exhibition and designed its catalogue: from treasured volumes of press-cuttings, he extracted quotations from old reviews and reprinted them beneath the titles of paintings, confident the criticism would look as dated and ridiculous to the modern reader as it had always appeared to him. Whistler was trying to force the change in public opinion that typically follows the death of a great artist, for he wanted both to witness the revolution in his lifetime and to laugh at his detractors.

Yet when the venture proved a brilliant success, prompting critics to revise their rulings and multiplying the value of his paintings, Whistler found cause for discontent. None of the exhibited works had been offered for sale, yet nearly half changed hands in the next twelve months as their owners rushed to profit from the conspicuous shift in taste. Whistler felt deeply offended that his "so-called friends" were suddenly so willing to part with their pictures.

He took small comfort in the consequent barrage of portrait commissions, wondering why they hadn't come in earlier years when he needed them badly and could have painted them just as well.[10] Indeed, the belated English appreciation of his work seems to have aggrieved Whistler more than outright neglect.

One of the paintings loosed from its moorings in the wake of the Goupil exhibition was *Variations in Flesh Colour and Green: The Balcony* (plate 1), which G. J. Cavafy had purchased many years earlier for the paltry sum of thirty guineas. Whistler had continued working on the picture even after its sale and claimed to have "more than quadrupled

Fig. 3. After Whistler's *Arrangement in Grey and Black: Portrait of the Artist's Mother* (Musée d'Orsay, Paris), ca. 1892. Photomechanical reproduction in halftone (15.5 x 17.3), 93.93. Signed by Whistler in the margin. Purchased by Freer from Wunderlich & Co., New York, on 20 November 1893. A copy of this photograph was shown at Whistler's retrospective held at the Goupil Gallery in 1892.

its value" as a result.[11] He himself once tried, and failed, to buy it back, but after its exhibition in 1892, Cavafy's son determined to sell it. Just as he was about to settle with J. C. Bancroft of Boston, Whistler intervened, and through an involved and underhanded process, he managed to obtain *The Balcony* and others of Cavafy's paintings for his agent in New York, Edward G. Kennedy of Wunderlich & Co.[12] Whistler's incentive was to secure one of the pictures for himself, but his stratagem had a providential outcome. *The Balcony* was purchased by Freer—who never expected, at the time, to be able to afford another Whistler painting— and thus came to be the cornerstone of his collection.

Freer let the artist know he had come into possession of *The Balcony* by way of a cablegram sent to inquire whether Whistler would permit *Harper's* to publish a reproduction of the painting (letter 13). This unexpected courtesy betokened Freer's enlightened opinion, from Whistler's point of view, that he was only the caretaker of those works by living artists he was fortunate enough to possess. Indeed, as Freer had recently informed another American painter, Thomas W. Dewing, he believed that the artist's wishes should control the works in which they held "joint ownership."[13] Whistler himself had always taken that position but until he met Freer had never known a patron willing to adopt it.

As guardian of the first important work by Whistler to enter an American collection, Freer was appalled to learn that while *The Balcony* was on display at the Society of American Artists' exhibition in New York, the wood panel on which it was painted had cracked. Fortunately, the damage could be repaired, but Freer remained too apprehensive to send the picture in 1893 to the World's Columbian Exposition in Chicago. Whistler would be represented there by a group of etchings and six oil paintings, three of which would later enter Freer's collection.[14] The display was the largest assemblage of his works yet shown in the United States, and the gold medal he was awarded was the first official honor granted him by his native country. Perhaps fearing that the absence of *The Balcony* had been noted with disapproval, Freer postponed sending Whistler his impressions for several months. The admiring letter he eventually composed would have defeated any doubts of his devotion (letter 14).

Until that success in Chicago, Whistler had been in no hurry, as he informed Freer in 1890, to "force himself on this side of the water" (appendix A). But six months after receiving Freer's compliments on his exhibition at the fair, Whistler signaled a change in attitude toward potential American patronage with a personal reply (letter 15); all previous correspondence had been handled by his wife. Whistler's affable letter promised new lithographs and a "pretty pastel," and it contained the casual acceptance of a commission proposed by Freer two years earlier. Freer had been thinking of a modest work in watercolor or pastel; Whistler offered an oil painting. In the new climate of appreciation, Freer had reason to worry whether he would be able to afford it, but in the end he paid just over a thousand guineas, approximately half what he had given Abbott Thayer the previous year for the picture called *A Virgin.*

Whistler had also extended a cordial invitation to Paris, where he and Beatrix had taken up residence in 1892, and Freer made a point of visiting that autumn on the first stage of his trip around the world. He was permitted to see much of Whistler's recent and unfinished work in his sixth-floor studio on the rue Notre Dame des Champs, where the commissioned painting, *Harmony in Blue and Gold: The Little Blue Girl* (plate 2), was already under way. Freer was given to understand that it would be completed and delivered to Detroit by the time he returned the following year. He purchased a watercolor painting and two pastels (letter 22) in addition to "specially choice impressions of twenty lithographs," some of them the first impressions Whistler printed (letter 20), which made his collection of Whistler prints incomparable.[15] Freer and Whistler discovered a shared

Fig. 4. *La Belle Dame Endormie* (w69), 1894. Lithograph (19.7 x 15.6), 06.183. This portrait of Beatrix Whistler is one of the lithographs that Freer purchased from Whistler in November 1894.

appreciation for Japanese woodblock prints—Freer was then on his way to Japan—and Whistler hypothesized that they were products of the decadent phase of a venerable artistic tradition, urging Freer to test the theory on his travels in Asia.[16]

To his close friend and business partner in Detroit, Frank J. Hecker, Freer wrote that Whistler had been "perfectly charming" in Paris, that he had braved a fearsome windstorm to call at his hotel and had twice invited him to lunch "at his beautiful little home" in the rue du Bac.[17] Thomas Dewing, who was enduring a period of expatriation in England, crossed the Channel to visit Freer, and with Whistler's friend the American sculptor Frederick MacMonnies, they made "a good sized party," Freer said, "and we amused ourselves greatly."[18] He had always enjoyed the company of artists, and in Paris that year Freer was given a glimpse of the bohemian life. MacMonnies dissuaded him from inviting all the American artists resident in Paris to a dinner in Whistler's honor—"they all hated one another," he said, "and would pass the evening more cheerfully by sticking forks into one another under the table"—so Freer decided, instead, to ask the American art students, "youngsters with their medals still to win." The party took place in the Latin Quarter, in an "old, curious, tumbledown restaurant," lasting from eight o'clock until nearly dawn. "Thirteen sat down," Freer reported to Hecker, "and later we wished that thirteen hundred might have been present to enjoy the sport." MacMonnies would recall that Freer had been visibly enchanted.[19]

For Whistler, too, those days held charm. He would have reason to remember them with special affection, for although his wife was ill, the gravity of her condition had not been disclosed (fig. 4). Freer made a romantic promise to send her a songbird from India, and through a happy coincidence of luck and effort he found the merles he wanted in the suburbs of Calcutta and was able to entrust them to a gallant sea captain (letter 25). The bird that survived the trip would give some solace and diversion to Beatrix as her cancer worsened and the Whistlers drifted between Paris and London, searching for hope. Whistler continued to work, producing a final group of lithographs that documents those despairing days in London (fig. 5), and probably taking up the commissioned work for Freer (*The Little Blue Girl*), which was to become, in his mind, poignantly associated with his wife's decline. She died in May of 1896, with the Indian bird singing her to sleep.

Freer must have sent Whistler a letter of condolence that has not survived, for the period of mourning following Beatrix Whistler's death is marked by a long pause in the correspondence. Yet Freer was aware that Whistler had moved into the home of his friend William Heinemann in Whitehall Court; that he had taken a studio at 8 Fitzroy Street, near Tottenham Court Road; and that the belligerent aspect of his character had resurfaced, probably as a symptom of grief. While Freer knew better than to make demands, he was growing impatient for the paintings and pastels he had purchased in 1894. When a business associate from Detroit, R. E. Plumb, went abroad in the autumn of 1896, Freer encouraged him to call on Whistler, suggesting that he compliment the Carlyle portrait if he found the artist in a hostile mood.[20] Freer's motive, of course, was to recover his possessions. His emissary managed to procure the watercolor painting and one of the pastels, and to buy on Freer's behalf virtually all the lithographs lately made in London and Lyme Regis (letter 28).

But *The Little Blue Girl* remained in England. When three more months passed without another word, Freer cabled Whistler to ask for it directly (letter 30)—an action he would deeply regret a few days later, when he received a letter Whistler had posted in London before his own peremptory cablegram had been dispatched from Detroit (letter 29). This anguished explanation of his failure to complete the painting conveyed Whistler's sorrow at parting with Beatrix; the flood of feeling extended to Freer, for whom the artist expressed his "warm feeling of affectionate appreciation." Freer would always hold the letter dear, labeling it "Very Important" and reading it aloud "with deep emotion" in later years to his friends Agnes Meyer and Louisine Havemeyer,[21] for it created a bond between the painter and his patron that transcended the terms of the commission. In reply, Freer pledged to guard *The Little Blue Girl* forever (letter 32).

Freer heeded the artist's implicit plea to leave him in peace with the painting. To Hecker he confided that he would not mind the waiting, "if I were only sure that in the event of Whistler's unlooked for death nothing would occur to the picture contrary to my interest."[22] His anxiety arose from Whistler's informal approach to accounts, which not only offended Freer's business practices but also caused him to worry that his possession of certain objects might be open to question. His correspondence with the artist reveals, for instance, that he remained uneasy about a Nocturne received in December 1896 until the following July, when Whistler finally got around to telling him its cost (letter 33). Freer promptly sent a check for the full amount, presenting it as a token payment—great works of art were beyond price, he said—and expressing his gratitude to Whistler for having entrusted the painting to his care (letter 34). Other

Fig. 5. *The Siesta* (w122), 1896. Lithograph (13.6 x 21.0), 05.99. Whistler released very few proofs of this lithograph, which pictures Beatrix ill at the Savoy Hotel in London, but he did present one copy to E. G. Kennedy as "La belle dame convalescente" (Whistler to Kennedy, 25 March 1896, Kennedy Papers, New York Public Library). When Freer saw it in New York, he considered it "possibly the greatest" of Whistler's lithographs and felt "perfectly sure that no other artist has ever approached it in lithography" (Freer to R. E. Plumb, 14 November 1896, FGA Letterpress Book 4). Failing to obtain an impression from the artist directly, Freer bought this print in 1905 from Wunderlich & Co. for $250, the highest price he ever paid for a lithograph.

patrons were not so accommodating. In a letter to an unco-operative purchaser, Whistler had written that in acquiring a work of art, the worthy patron "knows that he has the care of what really belongs to the world and to posterity."[23] It is little wonder, then, that the friendship between Whistler and Freer flourished.

Freer's credentials were rising in other respects as well. In 1899 he orchestrated the monopoly of the American railroad-car-building industry to create the American Car and Foundry Company and then retired, at the age of forty-five, to devote his time and abundant wealth to his art collection. That summer he purchased two examples of Whistler's latest work in oil (letter 37), in which he sensed a "dignity, amounting almost to solemnity, that keeps one while in its presence constantly reminded of the efforts of the early Greeks and Egyptians."[24] Those acquisitions would have confirmed, if further proof were needed, that Freer was not speculating in Whistlers; for although the artist himself considered his recent paintings the crowning achievements of his career—he told his biographers Joseph and Elizabeth Pennell that "all that had gone before was experimental"—they were not as highly valued on the market as his early works, which had come to be regarded as safe investments.[25]

With evidence of Freer's faith at hand, Whistler proposed a "mutually advantageous" arrangement of his own in a letter written from the French seaside resort near Dieppe where he was convalescing from influenza (letter 37). His idea, frankly stated, was that Freer should assemble the premier collection of his works. While it would have been tacitly understood that Whistler's proposal was impelled by respect for Freer's discriminating taste and acquisition record, the reason he gave for making it was simply Freer's nationality. The English, he said, had forfeited the chance to keep "a fine collection of Whistlers" in their country by continuing to sell "literally for thousands what they had gotten for odd pounds." An apposite example was *Nocturne: Blue and Silver—Bognor* (plate 3), which Freer was thinking of purchasing from Alfred Chapman who, if Whistler's recollection can be trusted, had paid no more for it than fifty pounds. Freer spent more than a thousand buying the Nocturne, leaving Chapman, in Whistler's estimation, "up to his armpits in ill-gotten wealth!—an offender at *first hand*—for the paintings he has turned over and over again, he originally had *from me direct!*"[26] Since for Whistler each sale of this sort meant a friendship betrayed, he was eager to seal his "communion" with Freer.

Whistler sent several tokens of his esteem to London, where Freer was staying that summer at the Carlton Hotel. First came a copy of his latest publication, *Eden versus Whistler: The Baronet and the Butterfly*, chronicling his quarrel with Sir William Eden (letter 37). Whistler's other gifts augured better relations. He delivered the second of the two pastels Freer had purchased in Paris, which according to an inscription in his hand on a sheet of hotel stationery was meant to be called *A Violet Note—Spring* (plate 4).[27] The title suggests a kinship with the commissioned oil painting (also intended, as Whistler said, "to, in a way, hint at 'Spring'"), as does the subject of a slender young nude with a white ceramic vase of flowers: *A Violet Note* is probably the "very pretty pastel" Whistler had mentioned in his first letter to Freer (letter 15). When the artist himself returned from Pourville-sur-Mer, he gave Freer an impression of a lithograph, *Confidences in the Garden* (fig. 6), picturing Beatrix and her sister Ethel in the garden at the rue du Bac; and probably the famous photogravure of the artist posing with characteristic panache (frontispiece), autographed and inscribed to Freer, "à un de ces jours"—until we meet again.

Fig. 6. *Confidences in the Garden* (w60), 1894. Lithograph printed in black ink on antique, cream-colored laid paper from a book (21.2 x 16.2), 06.176. Signed in pencil with the butterfly and inscribed by Freer, verso, "'Confidences.' / Given to me by Mr. Whistler, August 1899 / C.L.F." Freer had purchased another impression of this lithograph in November 1894.

In October 1900, when they met again in London, both were unwell (letter 41). Whistler's illness lingered into the winter, compelling an unfortunate trip to Corsica. Freer's had begun with overexertion in Paris, where he tried to see too much of the Exposition Universelle; his exhaustion was compounded

Fig. 7. Rosalind Birnie Philip, ca. 1903. Photograph by W. and D. Downey, London.

by crossing the Channel in a gale, which left him in a state of "nervous shock," torpid and depressed. "Besides," Freer wrote Hecker from London, "the weather here is hell."[28] He bought little that year, other than a villa on the isle of Capri, but by 1901 he was prepared to cooperate in Whistler's plan for the collection. The artist wrote an urgent letter informing Freer that John J. Cowan, an Edinburgh collector with whom he remained on amicable terms, was about to sell some of his paintings, and advising him to buy at least two of them at once (letter 54). Freer followed Whistler's instructions to the letter and within days the negotiations were complete. All three parties were pleased with the transaction, not only because they shared the belief that Whistler had never been "properly appreciated in England,"[29] but also because the friendly transfer had spared the paintings the indignities of the marketplace: when Freer notified Whistler's sister-in-law and amanuensis Rosalind Birnie Philip (fig. 7) that he had successfully closed the deal, he also assured her that the works would never be on the market again (letter 56).

Freer had assumed a ponderous responsibility, but Whistler had always been demanding of those who held his work. Over the years he had infuriated many a patron by summoning paintings for exhibitions as though they were his own. H. S. Theobald complained that when Whistler wanted to borrow some of the many works in his collection, the artist would simply send someone over with a note that read, "Please let bearer have fourteen of my pictures."[30] When Theobald once refused to comply, Whistler wrote to him indignantly: "It cannot be that you really mean to withhold pictures of mine from the recognition that the occasion of exhibition offers them, for the mere accidental reason that you happen to possess them." Freer, in contrast, fully appreciated the privilege of owning Whistler's works. As the model patron, he took every opportunity to spread the artist's fame, just as Whistler said Theobald should, and was "pleased and proud to do so."[31]

Even Freer's allegiance was tested when, in 1901, Whistler proposed to hold a Paris retrospective. He wrote from Ajaccio to ask Freer to lend for the occasion—as a "most charming act of friendship and courtesy & kindness"— virtually his entire collection (letter 44). Freer readily agreed to part with every painting but one: the Bognor Nocturne, which was already promised to exhibitions in New York City and Buffalo (letter 45). "I think he will content himself with what I am sending," Freer wrote to N. E. Montross, owner of the New York gallery, "and forgive the omission of 'Bognor.'"[32] Though the Paris exhibition would never come about, Whistler took up the matter of the absent Nocturne at the next opportunity, with the result that the painting would be reserved, in the future, for only those exhibitions the artist deemed worthy.[33] Freer was not altogether happy with the restriction, but he had by then resolved "never to do anything to disappoint Mr. Whistler in any way."[34]

Before the collection had even taken shape, Freer and Whistler seem to have reached an understanding regarding its characteristics: it would be the finest of its kind, it would reside in the United States, and it would never be dispersed. By the end of 1901, Freer's holdings of Whistler's work consisted of a group of prints and drawings, six oil paintings (not counting *The Little Blue Girl*), and a small number of watercolors and pastels—hardly a collection worthy of so imposing a scheme of preservation. Whistler probably

Fig. 8. Whistler in his studio at 86 rue Notre Dame des Champs, Paris, 1899. Photograph by M. Dornac.

intended to enlarge it substantially that summer, since he urged Freer to spend a few weeks with him going over the contents of his two studios (letter 49). When Freer could spare only three days in Paris, Whistler came over from London and, as Freer described it, took him in tow.[35] At the studio on rue Notre Dame des Champs (fig. 8), where Whistler rarely went after the death of his wife, Freer found several "very charming paintings, finished and unfinished." Most of them dated from 1893–94, the period preceding Beatrix's illness when Whistler was producing what appealed to Freer as "some of his most remarkable work." Although Freer very much wanted to buy something for the collection, Whistler would not be persuaded to part with a single painting. To each of Freer's gentle inquiries the artist would reply, "Yes, yes! Bye and bye. But to-day—oh, no! I cannot."[36]

The following summer, in 1902, Whistler agreed to relinquish four of the Paris pastels (though he insisted on keeping three of them another year to add some finishing touches) and a small oil painting he particularly prized, *Purple and Gold: Phryne the Superb!—Builder of Temples* (fig. 9), then on exhibition at the Grand Palais in Paris. Freer, as always, was eager to settle his account with Whistler, especially since he had not yet paid for several works obtained through the Company of the Butterfly, Whistler's short-lived commercial enterprise, or for the two paintings acquired in 1899. With the help of a "little note" from Rosalind Philip (letter 66), Freer fashioned an agreement that satisfied them both.[37] He would pay £2,000 (about $10,000) for the recent acquisitions and apply as credit against future purchases the sum he had paid in 1894 for *The Little Blue Girl,* which he designated still unpaid and "in progress for Mr. Freer" (letter 67). This financial sleight of hand was a compassionate gesture that technically restored to Whistler's possession the painting he could never give up.

Closing business with Whistler was but one of Freer's accomplishments that summer. He landed in Liverpool early in May and over the next seven weeks bought so many Whistlers that his "little group," as he customarily called his collection, took on entirely new dimensions. He more than doubled its size with a single purchase of thirty-one small oils, pastels, and watercolors—a collection he considered "undoubtedly the finest group" of its kind— from H. S. Theobald, the patron who had disappointed Whistler in the past.[38] Among Freer's other notable acquisitions was a painting bought at Whistler's urging, *The White Symphony: Three Girls* (fig. 10), one of a series called the Six Projects. When at length he concluded his negotiations with its owner, Whistler's estranged friend

Fig. 9. *Purple and Gold: Phryne the Superb!— Builder of Temples,* ca. 1898.Oil on panel (23.6 x 13.7), 02.115. Freer purchased this painting in 1902.

Fig. 10. *The White Symphony: Three Girls,* ca. 1868. Oil on millboard mounted on panel (46.4 x 61.6), 02.138.

and lithographic printer T. R. Way, Freer declared the purchase to be, in many ways, "the most important one artistically" he could have made of Whistler's works.[39]

Freer tried to keep the quantity of his acquisitions quiet, but he could not conceal the exhilaration he felt from spending so much money so well. "What I am picking up here is worth much more to me than Pressed Steel," he wrote to Hecker, instructing him to sell more stock to finance his purchases abroad—"a good name for my new findings would be pressed or compressed joy."[40] Yet the purpose of his visit was not only to buy Whistler's works but also to examine, for future reference, as many of his pictures as possible. Freer sent a lengthy "summary of news" to Hecker in Detroit, listing the beautiful places he had been, the delightful people he had met, and some of the important Whistlers he had been privileged to see, including the legendary Peacock Room. "At times," he said, "I wonder and wonder why all of this charm and joy should come into my little life!"[41]

Whistler insisted on painting Freer's portrait (plate 5) and regularly summoned him to the studio with instructions to bring a brown jacket (letter 61). Freer's modesty caused him to object at first, but he relented when he realized that the finished work would say more about the artist than the sitter. And the artist, Freer reported, was "in great feather" that summer, despite intermittent spells of illness;[42] Freer was undoubtedly the "rich American" mentioned by the Pennells, from whom an invitation to dinner could rouse Whistler from his bed and "cure him temporarily."[43] Whistler invited himself to dinner to celebrate the end of the Anglo-Boer War (letter 64); he ridiculed the English (his sympathies naturally resided with the Boers) and drank gin slings, Freer said, "till the lights went out."[44] Two weeks later Freer dined with Whistler at his new house in Cheyne Walk, near Chelsea Old Church (fig. 11). According to Elizabeth Pennell, the other guest that evening, Whistler delighted in showing off his Chinese porcelain—about which, she said, Freer "knew all the correct facts"—and extended the dinner with a bottle of burgundy and animated talk until almost eleven o'clock.[45]

Fig. 11. *Harmony in Brown and Gold: Old Chelsea Church*, ca. 1884. Oil on wood panel (8.90 x 14.8), 02.152. Whistler's last house in Chelsea was near the church pictured in this painting.

Clearly, Whistler was exhibiting his most vital aspect, and Freer may not have realized how precarious his friend's health had become. The night of the dinner party in Chelsea, Rosalind Philip confided to Elizabeth Pennell that persistent hammering from the construction next door was throwing Whistler into violent rages, "the thing above all others the Doctor cautioned them must be avoided."[46] That threat to his weak heart may have been a factor in the decision to make an excursion to Holland, but Freer informed Hecker that he and Whistler were going to escape the crowds and "senseless decorations" overwhelming London in the days leading to the coronation of Edward VII. "The only two sane men left," they departed the city on the twenty-first of June, hoping to find "quiet and reflection."[47] Freer seems to have been taken completely by surprise when, on the way to Amsterdam, Whistler suffered a serious heart attack.[48]

With Rosalind Philip and two servants, Freer accompanied Whistler to The Hague to find suitable accommodations and medical attention. Freer would remain there for more than a month, waiting for the artist to die. The doctor had been encouraging, but after nine days at Whistler's bedside, Freer abandoned hope. He was acutely conscious of his role as witness to a famous artist's final hours, and his sentimental letters from The Hague contrive a peaceful ending to a notoriously contentious life. Describing the supernal calm of the deathbed scene, he wrote to Hecker:

> In the still nights, the pale dawns and lingering evenings, to sit at his bedside, near the large window overlooking the Plein, and watch and listen as he whispers of what to him is the truth, life and peace. No bitterness, no remorse, no revenge against the hundreds who for thirty years waged war against the young knight, he who has so successfully borne his lance against them all—He bears no ill will, he wants no praise, no crown! Enough for him the mysterious spirit sounded by the mellow tones of the

distant bells, the sparrow on the near by branch, the warm mottled lily in the vase, the sympathetic touch of a friends hand—

Whistler had issued his "last commands" by the fourth of July, presumably to Rosalind Philip, his heir, and to Freer, the appointed guardian of his reputation.[49]

But Whistler did not die. After three agonizing weeks of illness he suddenly began to regain his health, and Freer, somewhat dazed by the unexpected turn of events, made plans to return to Detroit, hoping first to spend some time in Capri or a Dutch seaside resort recovering from his own "excessive nervousness."[50] He was reluctant to leave Whistler and his sisters-in-law Rosalind Philip and Ethel Whibley, who remained to nurse the artist back to health, because of the friendship that had "strangely grown up" among the four of them; but an alarming report of his brother's illness hastened his departure. "Now that we should choose new paths, he falters not," Freer wrote Hecker in the lofty style that distinguishes his letters from Holland, "but like an old-time knight errant, with frank heart, he awaits the leagues before him. I can simply wish him to win and then go."[51] As it happened, Freer missed the boat in Rotterdam and had to remain in Holland another day, prolonging the exchange of affectionate farewells. He had sent Whistler a gift of butterflies, which the artist thought worthy of a daimyo or a doge (letters 68 and 69).

Shortly after Freer left The Hague, word of Whistler's condition reached the London *Morning Post*, which published the news together with a précis of the artist's career. The report sounded to Whistler like an obituary, and he fired off one of his characteristic letters to the editor, suggesting that the "unmerited eulogy" be "put back into its pigeon-hole, for later on."[52] There would be other disturbing instances of what Whistler called the "ready wreath and quick biography," for publications about his life and art were beginning to appear more frequently in England and the United States. That October, for instance, Freer received a letter from Nancy Bell, author of a forthcoming monograph that promised to be, she said, "the most important work on Whistler which has yet been published." To her request for permission to reproduce works in his collection, Freer replied with his policy of leaving such decisions to the artists themselves,[53] and forwarded to Whistler copies of the correspondence (letter 77). Whistler had been thrilled to find Freer's letter in the mail, sending for Rosalind Philip to share the pleasure of reading it; but he was outraged by the note from Mrs. Bell. While the artist was railing against her insolence in taking on the project and proclaiming her expertise without "making the slightest reference to him and his wishes," Mrs. Pennell paid a visit to Cheyne Walk and tried to argue that anyone was entitled to write about him (she was, after all, preparing a biography of her own); but Whistler would not be reasoned with. He remained in a state of agitation until some days later, when William Heinemann found him writing a letter to the presumptuous author, his customary means of combat.[54]

All Freer would ever know of the episode was that Whistler had "highly approved" of his answer to Mrs. Bell.[55] Whistler must have realized that he would not long be able to vanquish such offenders himself, and he counted on Freer to control the presentation of his art. On two important occasions in 1903, Freer demonstrated that he could be as demanding, even as difficult, as the artist himself. Visiting an exhibition at the Pennsylvania Academy of the Fine Arts in Philadelphia, he was dismayed to see Whistler's works in what he considered an "inferior location." It was too late to do anything about it, but Freer registered his disapproval in a "vigorous verbal protest" to the director, Harrison S. Morris (letter 79). Reminding Freer that there could be "other views about fitting installation for such delicate and precious works," Morris subsequently explained that "what was done by a Hanging Committee consisting of personal friends of Whistler, and through our own initiative, was done with the single purpose of doing him honor and giving you acknowledgment for your gracious act."[56] Freer returned an arctic letter worthy of Whistler, assuring Morris that the "honor" extended by the Pennsylvania Academy would not readily be forgotten.[57]

Regretting the consequence of a late response to the Philadelphia exhibition, Freer took decisive action when he learned that Whistler's works had not been given the promised place of honor in a New York exhibition: he instantly withdrew them from the show. He might have understood placing John Singer Sargent's portrait of the president in the more desirable location, but he could not countenance works of lesser importance arrayed on walls that were meant for Whistlers (letter 79). Sensitive to the artist's excitable condition, Freer agreed with his friend Richard A. Canfield, who was then in London posing for his portrait (fig. 12), that the unfortunate affair at the Society of American Artists should be kept to themselves. But Canfield told Whistler what had happened in New York and instructed Freer to send an exhaustive account.[58] Freer wrote down "the whole story complete" and beseeched Whistler to let him know for "future guidance" whether he had erred in any way (letter 79). Once fully in command of the

Fig. 12. Henry Wolf (1852–1916), after Whistler's *Portrait of Richard A. Canfield* (Private collection). Wood engraving (26.0 x 16.2), 08.242. Presented to Freer by Canfield.

facts, Whistler conveyed his confidence in Freer (letter 80), and Freer took genuine delight in having accurately anticipated the artist's wishes (letter 81).

The Pennells blamed Freer for introducing such "unnecessary worries" into Whistler's life and even implied that the resulting agitation had contributed to his demise.[59] Yet every proof of Freer's dedication must have had a salutary effect on Whistler, alleviating at least a portion of his anxiety, and he was eager to see his friend again in the summer of 1903. Having been led to believe that Freer would be in London after the fifteenth of June, he sent greetings on the sixteenth to the Carlton Hotel, hoping to find him there (letter 83). But Freer was in Spain, and afterward in Paris; and though he must have known that Whistler would be waiting, he did not appear in London until the end of the month. Evidently, he was in no hurry to repeat the previous year's ordeal. From Canfield and Rosalind Philip he had heard that Whistler's health was deteriorating by degrees, and when he finally arrived in London, Freer wrote Hecker that although it was difficult to believe Whistler would "let himself go" that season, he had nothing hopeful to say about his condition, which worsened as the summer wore on.[60]

Yet in that final month of Whistler's life Freer enjoyed what he described to Howard Mansfield as "an experience of extreme interest and a lesson of rare importance."[61] Nearly every day he visited Whistler in Chelsea and whenever the artist had the strength, they went out together for fresh air and a change of scene. On July 16, Whistler seemed much better: that afternoon from half past three they enjoyed a leisurely drive through St. James's and Hyde Park. The next day Freer arrived at the house in Cheyne Walk ten minutes later than usual—he recorded the precise time in his pocket diary— only to find that Whistler had died five minutes before. Years later Freer would move back the clock in his memory, as he must have wished he could do at the time, and say he had been with the artist at the "very last moment" of his life.[62]

Freer remained at Cheyne Walk all that night and the following day, largely out of friendship to the "heroines" of Whistler's family who had honored him, he said, "with responsibilities of the gravest importance."[63] While Rosalind Philip was indisposed, Freer received the callers who came to pay their last respects, among them Joanna Hiffernan and Maud Franklin, former mistresses of Whistler's whose faces Freer knew from paintings; in recounting the day's events to Louisine Havemeyer, Freer reflected that Whistler's life had been "bound up in the love of three devoted women."[64] He also made the funeral arrangements and paid the expenses, and he served as one of six pallbearers—none of whom was English.[65] There was a small assembly at the service in the Chelsea Old Church, and if only Freer had been willing to address an audience he might have delivered a fitting eulogy. "Mr. Whistler's true self," he afterward wrote to Mansfield, "his real ideals, his natural instincts, his charity and his personal achievements are known to a few intimates only. And this is as he wished."[66]

Elizabeth Pennell observed that after Whistler's death, Freer wore "a rather professional air of grief."[67] It is possible that he had spent his emotion in The Hague, where imminent death aroused feelings more intense than those brought on by the actual event. Freer's letters to Hecker from 1903 lack the fervor of those from the previous year, and he concluded a comparatively detached account of Whistler's death with a curiously qualified hyperbole: "Need I say that in all things of perfect refinement of beauty the *greatest masters* are now all gone—at least all known masters."[68] The afterthought forecasts the future of his collection, when Whistler's works would become part of a broader scheme incorporating art from the Asian cultures Freer was just beginning to discover.

Before leaving England that summer, Freer helped Rosalind Philip settle Whistler's affairs. He himself had been asked by Whistler (probably in The Hague) to serve as

Fig. 13. Paul Cesar Helleu (1859–1927), *Portrait of Whistler*, 1897. Drypoint (33.6 x 25.3), 97.103. Helleu made this print while Whistler posed for Giovanni Boldini (1844–1931) and remained, it was said, in his very worst mood. To Freer, Helleu's drypoint conveyed "a closer subjective suggestion of Whistler the friend than does the original in oil by Boldini" (Freer to Whitney Warren, 13 March 1909, FGA Letterpress Book 27).

executor of the estate but had declined in favor of Miss Philip, with whom he formed a durable alliance to execute their mutual understanding of Whistler's will.[69] Freer's honorary status in the family might have given him an advantage in choosing from the works remaining in Whistler's studio, but the purchases he made in 1903 seem to have all been foreordained. He acquired, for example, the remaining Six Projects which, with *The White Symphony,* completed the ensemble; and he obtained the paintings listed in 1902 as "unfinished," including the long-awaited *Little Blue Girl,* which he was permitted to purchase for the second time. Freer was also buying paintings from other collections, knowing they would become more difficult to purchase in the years ahead. Explaining his need to liquidate assets, Freer wrote to Hecker that what he was buying was "surely beyond price. Some day: many days after bonds or anything else can serve me, others will be served, well served, intelligently served by my slight efforts of this year."[70]

Freer had hoped that upon Whistler's death certain stories might also be laid to rest, but most of the obituaries and personal reminiscences appearing in 1903 perpetuated an unflattering image. "The gentler side of Mr. Whistler's character seems to have been practically unknown to the many writers who have thus far busied themselves in a stumbling way with his work and life," Freer wrote Whistler's cousin Emma W. Palmer, lamenting that "so many false impressions have been, and still are, being scattered." Yet he did nothing to correct the record except to preserve certain documents, notably the Whistler letters published here, "for the future enlightenment of the many who are prejudiced against the master."[71] He trusted that once the "foolishness" had run its course, someone "properly qualified and thoroughly acquainted with the real man" would write about the Whistler he had known (fig. 13).[72] "In the meantime," he said, "those who care for real art should be content and take full delight in the undying charm of his work."[73]

For if the end of the artist's life concluded his biography, it initiated the process of immortalizing his name—or, as Freer phrased it, Whistler's death brought to an end only "the first chapter of a life which will be famous in the coming centuries."[74] The second chapter opened in 1904 with the Whistler Memorial Exhibition organized by the Copley Society of Boston (fig. 14). Freer believed it was "destined to be the most important exhibition ever given in this country," and he was accordingly generous with loans from his collection. The Society, in turn, deferred to him (and through him, to Rosalind Philip) on decisions about every detail, down to the design of the catalogue and the invitation, which Freer decreed "should follow Mr. Whistler's standards as fully as possible."[75] As expected, the exhibition inspired a public and critical reappraisal of Whistler's achievement, diverting attention from the anecdotes that were accumulating into a spurious biography. Heartened by such serious appreciation in America, Freer offered his collection to the nation.

Although the gift to the Smithsonian Institution would include hundreds of works of Asian art and a select group of paintings by contemporary American artists, it was primarily notable for the Whistlers, which numbered nearly nine

Fig. 14. Installation of Whistler paintings at the Memorial Exhibition in Boston, 1904. Photograph by Thos. E. Marr, Boston. Freer lent more than fifty works to the exhibition: *Harmony in Blue and Gold: The Little Blue Girl, The Thames in Ice,* and *Variations in Flesh Colour and Green: The Balcony* are shown in this photograph. The full-length portrait in the center, *Harmony in Red: Lamplight* (Hunterian Art Gallery, Glasgow), was Whistler's first portrait of Beatrix.

hundred at the time. Freer was to continue building and refining the collection until his death, but he stipulated that upon its transfer to the Smithsonian nothing was to be removed or added; nothing was to be lent for exhibition elsewhere; and nothing else was to be shown in the building he planned to construct for its display. Those ironclad conditions guaranteed that the artist's works would never again be on the market and ensured that they would never be displaced by inferior objects or shown in anything less than an honorable position in an aesthetically appropriate setting. The Smithsonian Regents, in whose hands the matter rested, attempted to negotiate more lenient terms, but Freer was adamant; and in 1906, following Theodore Roosevelt's intervention, the Institution accepted his unprecedented donation with all its provisions intact.[76]

By the time he died in 1919, Freer had largely reconstructed his collection. He had continued to acquire works by Whistler, raising the count to nearly thirteen hundred, but the collection as a whole had nearly quadrupled in size, with the vast majority of additions works of Asian art. "The Far Eastern objects in the collection have increased abundantly since Mr. Whistler passed on," Freer wrote to Rosalind Philip in 1918, justifying the modification of the scheme:

> Treasures then unknown have come to light and a few of the finest to our group, and I often wish that he could come and see them along with those of his own when they are installed in their lovely permanent home now nearing completion in Washington.

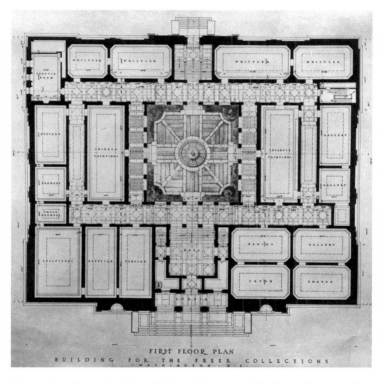

Fig. 15. First-floor plan, Freer Gallery of Art, 1923. The four galleries on the south side of the building were meant to be reserved for Whistler's works.

He assured her that four connecting galleries adjacent to the Peacock Room, set off from the others by a "spacious corridor," would be dedicated always and exclusively to Whistler's art (fig. 15).[77] The Asian objects were meant to enhance the Whistlers. As Agnes Meyer wrote, the collection as Freer had composed it was "an amplification of the spirit and intentions and artistic expression of his great friend. Probably no more complete and delicate tribute has ever been paid one man by another."[78]

Indeed, when the museum opened to the public in 1923, Whistler's influence was widely acknowledged. Yet it was Freer's name engraved above the portals. Having constructed and safeguarded "*the* collection" of Whistler's works, he ultimately claimed what the artist had promised the obliging patron, "the esteem and affection of history."[79]

Notes

1. Agnes Meyer, "The Charles L. Freer Collection," *Arts* 12 (August 1927): 67.

2. Mansfield described introducing Freer to Whistler's prints in "Charles Lang Freer," *Parnassus* 7 (October 1915): 16–18, 31. Accounts of Freer constructing his Whistler collection are included in Thomas Lawton and Linda Merrill, *Freer: A Legacy of Art* (Washington, D.C.: Freer Gallery of Art, 1993), 31–57; and David Park Curry, *James McNeill Whistler at the Freer Gallery of Art* (Washington, D.C.: Freer Gallery of Art, 1984), 11–33.

3. Freer to Alfred H. Granger, 14 May 1900, FGA Letterpress Book 6.

4. Beatrix Whistler to Edward G. Kennedy, 29 September 1889, quoted in Katharine A. Lochnan, *The Etchings of James McNeill Whistler* (New Haven: Yale University Press, 1984), 253. Freer's and Mansfield's etchings were shown in 1890 at the Grolier Club; other lenders to that exhibition were the prominent New York collectors Samuel P. Avery and Henry O. Havemeyer. See Frances Weitzenhoffer, *The Havemeyers: Impressionism Comes to America* (New York: Abrams, 1986), 55.

5. Freer to Emma W. Palmer, 17 February 1905, FGA Letterpress Book 16.

6. For example, Freer wrote to Howard Mansfield (3 March 1893, FGA

Letterpress Book 1): "I wonder when Whistler intends to send my impressions of the Venetian plates. Have you heard from him recently? I have not. He has several of my orders still unfilled. I presume some day however the things will come."

7. The unsigned pen-and-ink drawing is in the collection of the Hunterian Art Gallery at the University of Glasgow.

8. Elizabeth R. Pennell and Joseph Pennell, *The Life of James McNeill Whistler* (Philadelphia: Lippincott, 1908), 2:116. Unless otherwise indicated, all subsequent citations are from this edition.

9. Whistler to Henry Studdy Theobald, 25 April 1888, Department of Prints and Drawings, British Museum, London.

10. Pennell and Pennell, *Life of Whistler,* 2:126.

11. Whistler to John Cavafy (G. J. Cavafy's son), [May 1879], typescript copy, GUL Whistler C50.

12. See William B. Sieger, "Whistler and John Chandler Bancroft," *Burlington Magazine* 136 (October 1994): 675–82.

13. Freer to Dewing, 7 June 1892, FGA Letterpress Book 1.

14. Freer would acquire *Blue and Silver—Trouville,* 02.137, in 1902, *La Princesse du pays de la porcelaine,* 03.91, in 1903, and *Nocturne: Blue and Gold—Valparaiso,* 09.127, in 1909.

15. Freer to Frank J. Hecker, from Paris, 16 November 1894, FGA Hecker.

16. Agnes E. Meyer, *Charles Lang Freer and His Gallery* (Washington, D.C.: Freer Gallery of Art, 1970), 5.

17. Freer to Hecker, from Paris, 16 November 1894, FGA Hecker.

18. Freer to Dwight W. Tryon, from the SS *Natal* en route to Ceylon, 9 December 1894, typescript copy, Nelson C. White Papers, Archives of American Art, Smithsonian Institution, Washington, D.C.

19. Freer to Hecker, from Paris, 16 November 1894, FGA Hecker; Pennell and Pennell, *Life of Whistler,* 2:152. In recounting his story to the Pennells, MacMonnies referred to Freer as "a millionaire friend of Whistler's and mine" and to Dewing as "a distinguished American painter, who sat opposite to Whistler, and who was much respected by the youth."

20. Freer to Plumb, 16 October 1896, FGA Letterpress Book 3.

21. Meyer, *Charles Lang Freer,* 7–8; Louisine W. Havemeyer, *Sixteen to Sixty: Memoirs of a Collector,* ed. Susan Alyson Stein (New York: Urus Press, 1993), 212. Mrs. Meyer remarked that the letter "tells more about the two men, the quality of their friendship and the reason why, in a sense, the whole Freer Gallery of Oriental art is dedicated to Whistler, than anything I could add.

It is the finest proof we have that the quarrelsome Whistler, the author of 'The Gentle Art of Making Enemies,' was not the ruthless man he seemed, but was reacting to the severely critical attacks on his new artistic techniques with the natural impatience of an overly sensitive human being" (p. 8).

22. Freer to Hecker, from London, 28 July 1899, FGA Hecker.

23. Whistler to Theobald, 25 April 1888, British Museum.

24. Freer to William K. Bixby, 7 November 1900, FGA Letterpress Book 7.

25. Pennell and Pennell, *Life of Whistler,* 2:203.

26. Whistler to John J. Cowan, 6 January 1900, GUL Whistler C239.

27. Freer to Hecker, from London, 28 July 1899, FGA Hecker. The note in Whistler's hand on Carlton Hotel letterhead is bound into Freer's autograph copy of *The Baronet and the Butterfly* (Paris, 1899) in the Rare Books Collection, FGA Library.

28. Freer to Hecker, from London, 16 October 1900, FGA Hecker.

29. Cowan to Freer, 9 November 1901, FGA Cowan.

30. Pennell and Pennell, *Life of Whistler,* 2:128.

31. Whistler to Theobald, 25 April 1888, British Museum.

32. Freer to Montross, 11 March 1901, FGA Letterpress Book 7.

33. Freer to William T. Evans, 11 November 1901, FGA Letterpress Book 8.

34. Freer to R. A. Canfield, 25 February 1903, FGA Letterpress Book 10.

35. Freer to Lendall Pitts, 13 August 1901, FGA Letterpress Book 8. Freer wrote to apologize for failing to see Pitts again in Paris, as planned, explaining that Whistler "remained up to the hour of my departure . . . and he and several other mutual friends took up my time completely."

36. Freer to H. H. Benedict, 28 November 1901, Freer Letterpress Book 8.

37. Freer to Hecker, from London, 20 June 1902, FGA Hecker. "I have settled most amicably with Mr. Whistler," Freer wrote, "Good!! Of course, for things, by him, still unfinished a settlement some other year will follow."

38. Freer to Hecker, from London, 3 June 1902, FGA Hecker. Whistler had assumed that Theobald's "beautiful things" would always be with him, as he said, "like the poor!" (Whistler to Theobald, 25 April 1888, British Museum).

39. Freer to Hecker, from The Hague, 17 July 1902, FGA Hecker.

40. Ibid., 13 June 1902.

41. Ibid., 30 May 1902.

42. Ibid., 6 May and 13 June 1902.

43. Elizabeth R. Pennell and Joseph Pennell, *The Life of James McNeill Whistler,* 5th ed. (Philadelphia: Lippincott, 1911), 354.

44. Freer to Hecker, 3 June 1902, FGA Hecker.

45. Elizabeth R. Pennell and Joseph Pennell, *The Whistler Journal* (Philadelphia: Lippincott, 1921), 241. The dinner was held on 17 June 1902.

46. Pennell and Pennell, *Whistler Journal,* 241.

47. Freer to Hecker, from London, 20 June 1902, FGA Hecker.

48. Ibid., from The Hague, 27 June 1902.

49. Ibid., 4 July 1902.

50. Ibid., 11 July 1902.

51. Ibid., 28 July 1902.

52. Letter to the editor, "Latest Bulletin from Mr. Whistler," *Morning Post* (London), 6 August 1902.

53. Nancy Bell to Freer, 18 September 1902, copy, GUL Whistler B46; Freer to Bell, 14 October 1902, FGA Letterpress Book 9 (copy, GUL Whistler F467).

54. Pennell and Pennell, *Whistler Journal,* 258–59. The episode, which occurred on 27 and 28 October 1902, is also discussed in Pennell and Pennell, *Life of Whistler,* 2:296.

55. Philip to Freer, 5 December 1902, FGA Philip. Nancy Bell's book, *James McNeill Whistler,* part of Bell's Miniature Series of Painters, would be published by George Bell & Sons, London, in 1904, with a reproduction of *The Thames in Ice,* plate 14.

56. Morris to Freer, 2 March 1903, copy, GUL Whistler P271.

57. Freer to Morris, 14 March 1903, FGA Letterpress Book 11. The Pennells were certain Freer had misjudged the exhibition: for their account see *Life of Whistler,* 2:297–98.

58. Freer to Canfield, 21 March 1903; J. M. Kennedy to Freer, 23 March 1903, FGA Letterpress Book 11.

59. Pennell and Pennell, *Life of Whistler,* 2:297–98.

60. Freer to Hecker, from London, 12 July 1903, FGA Hecker.

61. Freer to Mansfield, 20 August 1903, FGA Letterpress Book 11.

62. Freer to Whitney Warren, 13 March 1909, FGA Letterpress Book 27.

63. Havemeyer, *Sixteen to Sixty,* 212–13; Freer to Hecker, from London, 22 July 1903, FGA Hecker.

64. Havemeyer, *Sixteen to Sixty,* 213.

65. Pennell and Pennell, *Whistler Journal,* 297. According to the ledgers of Messrs. Banting of St. James's, the Crown Undertakers, Freer spared no expense in Whistler's funeral and burial in Chiswick: the total cost was £88.1.10 (thanks to Claire Gapper of the Old Chiswick Protection Society).

66. Freer to Mansfield, 20 August 1903, FGA Letterpress Book 11.

67. Pennell and Pennell, *Whistler Journal,* 293.

68. Freer to Hecker, from London, 18 July 1903, FGA Hecker.

69. Freer to Fullerton L. Waldo, 16 April 1910, FGA Letterpress Book 30.

70. Freer to Hecker, from London, 12 July 1903, FGA Hecker.

71. Freer to Palmer, 9 March 1905, FGA Letterpress Book 16.

72. Ibid., 17 February 1905, FGA Letterpress Book 16; and 6 September 1904, FGA Letterpress Book 14.

73. Freer to Mansfield, 20 August 1903, FGA Letterpress Book 11.

74. Freer to Hecker, from London, 22 July 1903, FGA Hecker.

75. Freer to Holker Abbott, president of the Copley Society, 17 December 1903, FGA Exhibitions/Copley Society. The exhibition catalogue, published in two parts, was designed in imitation of Whistler's brown-paper pamphlets, and the invitation to the opening reception was adorned with a Whistler butterfly. Copies of these documents are in the Rare Books Collection, FGA Library.

76. For an account of Freer's gift to the nation, see Lawton and Merrill, *Freer,* 177–201.

77. Freer to Philip, 22 July 1918, GUL Whistler F528.

78. Meyer, "Freer Collection," 67–69.

79. Whistler to Theobald, 25 April 1888, British Museum.

Editorial Note

In translating handwritten letters into published correspondence, an editor necessarily suppresses certain idiosyncrasies. Whistler's letters are particularly difficult to capture in print, as they are little works of art in themselves, with eloquent dashes and spirited exclamations as well as expansive spaces marking pauses between paragraphs. Freer's, in contrast—and in keeping with his character—appear conventional and composed, yet they show lapses in spelling and grammar that hint of his humble background. I have preserved as much as possible of the original text, leaving the writer's syntax, spelling, capitalization, and changes of heart intact. I have also attempted to preserve punctuation, which alternates between expressive and ambiguous; I added punctuation only when it appeared to have been accidentally omitted—at the end of a paragraph or parenthetical statement or quotation. All other editorial insertions and conjectures are enclosed in square brackets or notes.

Transcriptions, unless otherwise noted, are from the addressees' copies and signed by the correspondent; Whistler's butterfly signatures have been reproduced. Addresses from letterhead stationery are considered part of the letter. A note at the foot of each letter gives the location of the holograph and contemporary copies, together with information provided by the envelope, when it survives, the type of stationery, and details of previous publication.

American equivalents for British currency are given in 1890s dollars, as noted in Freer's records. A guinea equals one pound, one shilling; twenty shillings make a pound.

Illustrated works are in the collections of the Freer Gallery of Art, Smithsonian Institution. Dimensions are given in centimeters, with height preceding width. Whistler's etchings are identified by their number in Edward G. Kennedy's catalogue, lithographs by their number in T. R. Way's catalogue; all Freer Gallery works are identified by their accession numbers. The following abbreviations are used throughout:

FGA   Freer Gallery of Art, Smithsonian Institution, Washington, D.C. Charles Lang Freer Papers.

GUL   Glasgow University Library, Special Collections.

K   Kennedy, Edward G. *The Etched Work of Whistler.* New York: The Grolier Club, 1910. Reprint, Alan Wofsy Fine Arts, 1978.

W   Way, T. R. *Mr. Whistler's Lithographs: The Catalogue.* 2d ed. London: George Bell & Sons, and New York: Wunderlich & Co., 1905.

Plate 1

Variations in Flesh Colour and Green: The Balcony
1864–70. Oil on panel (61.4 x 48.8), 92.23.

Plate 2

Harmony in Blue and Gold: The Little Blue Girl
1894–1903. Oil on canvas (74.7 x 50.5), 03.89.
Frame designed by the artist.

Plate 3

Nocturne: Blue and Silver—Bognor

1871–76. Oil on canvas (50.3 x 80.3), 06.103.

Plate 4

A Violet Note—Spring

ca. 1894–99. Pastel on brown paper (27.6 x 18.1), 94.26.

Plate 5

Portrait of Charles Lang Freer

1902. Oil on panel (51.8 x 31.7), 03.301.

Plate 6

Harmony in Blue and Violet

ca. 1890. Pastel on brown paper (28.0 x 18.0), 90.8.
Signed and inscribed by Whistler, verso, "Harmony in Blue & Violet."

Plate 7

The Embroidered Curtain

(K410), 1889. Etching, fourth state, printed in brown ink on
cream-colored laid paper (23.9 x 16.0), 06.126.

Plate 8

Blue and Gold—The Rose Azalea

ca. 1890–95. Watercolor on brown paper (27.8 x 18.1), 94.25.

Plate 9

Rose and Red: The Little Pink Cap

1890s. Pastel on brown paper (27.9 x 18.4), 94.27.

Plate 10

Nocturne in Black and Gold: Entrance to Southampton Water
ca. 1875–76. Oil on canvas (47.6 x 62.3), 97.21.

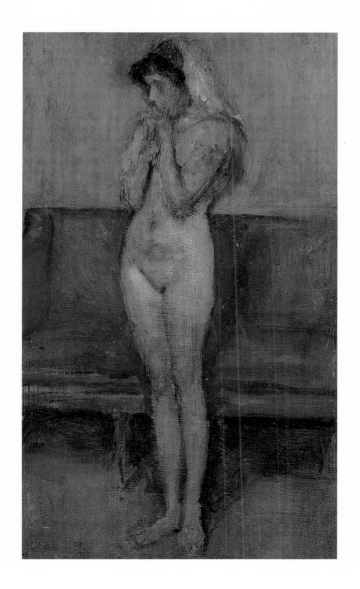

Plate 11

Rose and Brown: La Cigale

1899. Oil on panel (21.7 x 12.6), 02.110.

Plate 12

Rose and Gold: The Little Lady Sophie of Soho
1898–99. Oil on canvas (64.5 x 53.5), 02.109.

Plate 13
Chelsea Children
mid-1880s. Watercolor on paper (12.7 x 21.6), 02.116.

Plate 14

The Thames in Ice

1860/64. Oil on canvas
(74.6 x 55.3), 01.107.

Plate 15

Rose and Silver: Portrait of Mrs. Whibley

early 1890s. Watercolor on paper
(28.2 x 18.8), 01.108.

Plate 16

Nocturne: Blue and Silver—Battersea Reach

ca. 1878. Oil on canvas (49.9 x 76.5), 02.97.

/ Letter from Freer to Whistler

Peninsular Car Co.
Detroit, Mich.
Mar. 31st 1890—

Dear Mr. Whistler,

I arrived home two weeks ago to day and brought through safely with me the etchings for Mr. Mansfield and myself, also that charming pastel and that very interesting frame—for all of which I am under many obligations to you.[1]

My visit with yourself and Mrs. Whistler[2] was the event of my trip, and I shall long have reason to remember most pleasantly the hospitality you both bestowed—When you come to America you must surely visit Detroit and give me an opportunity to reciprocate your kindness—

The N.Y. Tribune has already mentioned your Amsterdam etchings—I sent you a copy of the newspaper.[3]

Next week an important exhibition of your work consisting of a selection of your etchings, watercolors, and pastels, from the period of "Little Venice" including the ten Amsterdam prints is to be held in the new Club house of The Grolier Club in N.Y. City.[4] It will undoubtedly attract much attention—

I send you under seperate cover a copy of yesterdays "Free Press" containing an article which I very much regret is not in better shape—It came to be published by reason of a short address which I delivered before the Witenagemote Club of this city last week—At which time I exhibited a selection of your earliest and latest etchings and refered to my recent visit with you. A reporter of The Detroit Free Press was present and asked for an interview which I granted with the understanding that his article would be given to me for correction before publication.[5] This I am sorry to say was not done hence the blunders—I hope you will overlook them.

With cordial greetings to Mrs Whistler and yourself, I remain

Respectfully yours
Charles L. Freer
77 Alfred St.
Detroit. Mich.

GUL Whistler F432. Company letterhead.

---

1. Freer purchased ten of Whistler's Amsterdam etchings for himself and seven on behalf of Howard Mansfield (1849–1938), the New York attorney whose print collection had afforded Freer's introduction to Whistler's etchings; the impressions Freer acquired are listed in appendix B. The pastel drawing he bought is *Harmony in Blue and Violet,* plate 6.

2. Beatrix Whistler (1855–1896) was the daughter of the sculptor John Birnie Philip (1824–1875) and Frances Black Philip (1825/26–1917) and the widow of Whistler's friend, the architect E. W. Godwin (1833–1886). She and Whistler married in August 1888.

3. "Whistler's Etchings," *New-York Daily Tribune,* 24 March 1890 (FGA Whistler Scrapbook 1:4). The article refers to Whistler's "recent Holland etchings" in the possession of "two American amateurs, one residing in New York and the other in Detroit."

4. The etching *Little Venice* (K183) 1879–80 was published as part of Whistler's "First Venice Set" in 1881. The Grolier Club, founded in 1884 for the study and appreciation of the arts of the book, also held occasional exhibitions of works on paper.

5. The Witenagemote was a gentlemen's club interested in promoting the arts in Detroit. The article adapted from Freer's address is reprinted in appendix A.

Fig. 16. *Nocturne: Dance-House* (K408), 1889. Etching, first state (27.1 x 16.8), 06.117.

2 Letter from Freer to Whistler

Peninsular Car Co.
Detroit, Mich.
April 28th, 1890

My dear Mr. Whistler,

An evening or two ago my business partner and partic-ular friend Mr. Frank J. Hecker,[1] of this city, spent several hours at my home enjoying my portfolios of your work. Many of them he had seen before, but the Amsterdam plates were of course new to him. They completely charmed him and he requested me to if possible, secure copies for him of all those I have,[2] viz;—

		Guineas
1	Pierrot	15
2	Long House (The Dyers)	12
3	Zaandam	10
4	Steps[3]	12
5	The Mill	12
6	The Square House	12
7	The Dance House (Nocturne)[4]	15
8	The Balcony	15
9	The Little Drawbridge[5]	10
10	The Bridge	12

During our recent conversation you will perhaps remem-ber that I expressed a desire hereafter to purchase your work direct from yourself. To this you kindly assented. Such an arrangement should be mutually advantageous.

Now then, will you be good enough to send me the ten prints herein before named by book post. They will come through safely if put between heavy card boards—and addressed,

Mr. Charles L. Freer.
77 Alfred St.
Detroit, Michigan.
U.S.A.

Fig. 17. *Little Drawbridge, Amsterdam*
(κ412), 1889. Etching, first state (17.6 x
12.7), 06.115.

By the way, I have just received word from N.Y. of the arrival there of another new etching by you entitled "The Lace Curtain"[6] will you be so kind as to send me one, choosing a good impression and writing my name on the back, also kindly send proofs for me of any more new plates you may have made since I was at your studio. I presume Mr. Mansfield has written you about the charming exhibition of your work recently made at the Grolier Club in New York. All ten of the ~~plates~~ prints herein named were shown—Also that delightful pastel which you kindly let me have.[7] Many N.Y. artists attended the exhibition and were particularly delighted with your latest work—

With cordial greetings to Mrs. Whistler, I remain

Sincerely yours,
Charles L. Freer

P.S. Kindly send me bill for etchings as soon as forwarded and I will at once remit draft on London—

GUL Whistler F433. Company letterhead. Envelope addressed to Whistler at Tower House, Tite Street, Chelsea, London; postmarked Detroit, 29 April 1890.

---

1. Frank J. Hecker (1846–1927), president of the Peninsular Car Company and Freer's neighbor in Detroit.

2. See appendix B.

3. *Steps, Amsterdam* (K403), fig. 1.

4. *Nocturne: Dance-House* (K408), fig. 16.

5. *Little Drawbridge, Amsterdam* (K412), fig.17.

6. One of the Amsterdam etchings of 1889, subsequently retitled *The Embroidered Curtain* (K410): see letter 5.

7. *Harmony in Blue and Violet,* plate 6.

♪ Letter from Beatrix Whistler to Freer

21, Cheyne Walk.[1]
Chelsea.
[15 May 1890]

Dear Mr Freer.

Mr Whistler is so very much occupied at this moment, that I am writing this for him, to thank you for your kind letter.

I have sent you today the etchings for Mr. Hecker.

I have included two trial proofs of the "Lace Curtain." If you remember, you saw it. They are early proofs—when the plate is completed you can exchange them for others, if you wish.[2]

Wunderlich has one or two of them.

The proof of "The Mill" is the last one of that state of the plate; and I find there is not a proof of the Nocturne with the figures.[3] However Mr. Hecker can return it, when Mr. Whistler prints some more.

Thank you very much for the cuttings you sent—who is Mr Hitchcock? Is he the painter?[4] Mr Whistlers book will be out very soon—you must look out for it.[5]

With kindest regards from us both

Believe me

Very sincerely—
Beatrix Whistler.

FGA Beatrix Whistler 271 (draft, GUL Whistler W583). Personal stationery. Envelope addressed to Freer at 77 Alfred Street, Detroit; postmarked Chelsea, 15 May 1890, and Detroit, 27 May 1890; with a notation in Freer's hand, "ans."

1. The Whistlers moved from Tower House, Tite Street, to 21 Cheyne Walk, shortly after Freer's visit in March.

2. *The Embroidered Curtain* (K410), plate 7. Freer appears to have kept this impression, which is in the fourth state.

3. Freer's impressions of *The Mill* (K413), 06.127, and *Nocturne: Dance-House* (K408), fig. 16, are in the first state: see appendix B. In the second state of *Nocturne: Dance-House,* the figures in the window have been almost burnished out of the picture.

4. Probably J. Ripley Hitchcock (1857–1918), author of *Etching in America* (New York: White, Stokes & Allen, 1886) and, presumably, of the *New-York Daily Tribune* review Freer had sent Whistler (see Freer to J. H. Jordan, 27 March 1890, FGA Vouchers). Beatrix Whistler refers to the American painter George Hitchcock (1850–1913).

5. *The Gentle Art of Making Enemies: As Pleasingly Exemplified in Many Instances, wherein the Serious Ones of This Earth, Carefully Exasperated, Have Been Prettily Spurred on to Unseemliness and Indiscretion, while Overcome by an Undue Sense of Right,* a compendium of Whistler's writings on art, was published by William Heinemann, London, in June 1890 (fig. 18).

Fig. 18. Illustration for *The Gentle Art of Making Enemies,* 1890. Crayon with white gouache on paper (25.3 x 23.1), 04.90.

✐ Letter from William Bell to Freer

21, Cheyne Walk,
Chelsea.
May 17, 1890

Sir

I am directed to enclose account.

Yours Truly
William Bell[1]

To C. L. Freer. Esq.

[enclosure]

C. L. Freer Esq.
May 15 1890
1. The Lace Curtain. £12.12.0[2]

FGA Bell. Whistler's personal stationery. Notation on account in red pencil
in another hand, "K410." Envelope addressed to Freer at 77 Alfred Street,
Detroit; postmarked Chelsea, 17 May 1890, and Detroit, 25 May 1890.

---

1. William Bell was Whistler's personal secretary from early 1890 probably
through most of 1891.

2. *The Embroidered Curtain* (K410), plate 7.

✒ Letter from Beatrix Whistler to Freer

21, Cheyne Walk.
Chelsea.
[11 July 1890]

Dear Mr. Freer

Thank you so much for your kind letter. It was so nice of you [to] tell your friend I admired his work. I shall be pleased to have the engraving.

Mr. Whistler who is very much occupied just now, wishes me to say how pleased he is you like the proofs, and when there is another state of the "Embroidered Curtain"[1] he will only be too happy to change the proof you at present have.

We have had a visit from Mr. Carter whom we found most interesting.[2] He has gone to Paris but promised to return, which I hope will be before we go away, which we intend doing very shortly—either to Spain or Venice in search of more pictures which we hope to show you on your next visit to England.

With our kindest regards
Believe me

Very sincerely yours
Beatrix Whistler

[enclosure]

June 16 1890
Received of Charles L Freer Esq the sum of One Hundred and Fifty Six Pounds Nine Shillings (£156-9.0) in payment of Etchings delivered.

Beatrix Whistler

FGA Beatrix Whistler 273. Personal stationery. Probably sent in envelope (FGAWhistler 272) addressed to Freer at 77 Alfred Street, Detroit; postmarked Chelsea, 11 July 1890; with a notation in Freer's hand, "ans."

1. *The Embroidered Curtain* (K410), plate 7.

2. Probably Walter S. Carter, a Brooklyn lawyer who actively collected Whistler prints from 1888 until his death in 1904; Mansfield had provided his introduction to the artist. See M. Lee Wiehl, *A Cultivated Taste: Whistler and American Print Collectors* (Middletown, Conn.: Davison Art Center, Wesleyan University, 1983), 9 and 13. Carter's collection of sixty-three Whistler etchings would be auctioned in New York in February 1905: Freer wrote to his friend Margaret Watson (later Margaret Parker; 1867–1936) that he had examined Carter's prints at the time of their purchase and particularly recalled the Amsterdam proofs, which he thought "worthy of the highest praise" and predicted would bring a high price at auction (21 February 1905, FGA Letterpress Book 16). As it happened, Carter's impression of *Balcony, Amsterdam* (K405) fetched an unprecedented $875 (*New York Sun*, 26 February 1905, FGA Whistler Scrapbook 1:12).

Fig. 19. *The Garden* (W38), 1891. Lithograph (17.0 x 18.2), 06.161. One of the lithographs Whistler sent to Freer in January 1892, *The Garden* depicts a gathering of the Whistlers' friends and relations in the garden of 21 Cheyne Walk.

6 Letter from Beatrix Whistler to Freer

21, Cheyne Walk.
Chelsea.
[25 July 1890]

Dear Mr. Freer.

Will you tell Mr. Church how pleased we both are with his beautiful picture, which arrived safely. It is a most charming fancy—and I admire it exceedingly.[1] It is wonderfully engraved—we can do nothing like it here. When the house is finished (at present it is full of painters) I shall give it a place of honour in the drawing room.

The book is published I believe some days ago in America—and the publishers have ordered another edition to be printed at once[2]—so I was surprised you had not seen it—I wish you would send us some of your fine weather you speak of—it has rained without ceasing all through last month and this, and we begin to wonder where we shall find the pictures this year as we see it is predicted that next month the rain fall is to measure four inches?!

I have written so many letters this month that I cannot remember if I acknowledged your letter with the cheque. My impression is that I did—but if I did not you must forgive me. I hope your friend is pleased with his proofs. I thought they were beauties.

With our kindest regards
Believe me

Very sincerely
Beatrix Whistler

FGA Beatrix Whistler 272. Personal stationery. Probably sent in envelope (FGA Beatrix Whistler 273) addressed to Freer at 77 Alfred Street, Detroit; postmarked Chelsea, 25 July 1890, and Detroit, (?) July 1890.

---

1. Probably an engraving after a painting in Hecker's collection, *The Fog* (Detroit Institute of Arts, Michigan) by Freer's friend Frederick Stuart Church (1826–1900); Church had written Freer on 16 June 1890 that he would send him an additional proof of the engraving (FGA Church), presumably for the Whistlers.

2. The first American edition of Whistler's *Gentle Art* was published in July 1890 by John W. Lovell & Co., New York. The second, enlarged, "New Edition" was published later that year by Heinemann in London and G. P. Putnam's Sons in New York.

7 Letter from Freer to Whistler

[77 Alfred Street,
Detroit]
February 20th, 1891

My dear Mr. Whistler,

After several months of practically continuous absence from Detroit, I am again at home and spent last evening in reading to some friends who called, extracts from The Whirlwind on the thrashing you gave that fellow Moore.[1] I congratulate you upon scalping one more coward and trust that strength will be given you to continue your good work—

I thank you very much for sending me the copies of The Whirlwind and regret very much that my absence from home prevented an earlier acknowledgement of your kindness—

I am anxious to possess complete files of this crisp journal, particularly the numbers containing your illustrations

and have today sent my subscription for two years beginning with this first issue.[2]

About two years ago I purchased in New York a set
of your lithographs published by Way,[3] ~~and~~ also nine copies
of lithographs by you of street scenes and figures which I
was told you had never published except in very limited
number.[4] These pictures have given a great deal of pleasure
to myself and friends and I have given two or three impressions to artist friends—which I would like to replace. Can
I purchase from you one complete set of the nine unpub-
lished lithographs for an appreciative friend, also duplicates
of the figure pieces to replace those given from [my] own
collection? If you can let me have them, please forward
by mail at your early convenience, and send bill—I will
remit promptly—

Have you done any etching since my delightful visit to
your studio? If you have made any new plates, I earnestly
hope that you have kept good impressions for me, and, if
any are ready you will further favor me by sending them
with the lithographs. Am I asking too much?

I wish I could tell you how much genuine pleasure
and instruction your Amsterdam plates have given both
artists and amateurs throughout America—The impressions
I brought over for Mr. Mansfield and myself have been
exhibited a number of times and have left the very strongest
possible influence for good upon all those whose "appreciation is entertaining."

Did you make the proposed visit to Spain? Many of
your friends in this country are so glad that you went to
Holland and etched those wonderful plates—It gives us an
opportunity to see you at your best along side of Rembrandt,
with like subjects for comparison—I should think that you
would find very much in Spain to inspire and fascinate
you—and that a trip to that charming country would lead to
your doing for Spain what you have already so magnificently
done for Holland—

Trusting that yourself and Mrs. Whistler are enjoying the best of health, and with cordial greetings, I remain,

Sincerely yours,
Charles L. Freer
77 Alfred St.
Detroit.
Michigan.

GUL Whistler F434.

---

1. *The Whirlwind: A Lively and Eccentric Newspaper,* a weekly London periodical, printed commentary and correspondence pertaining to some uncomplimentary and allegedly libelous remarks about the late E. W. Godwin, Whistler's friend and Beatrix Whistler's first husband, published in *The Hawk*. Whistler had retaliated in September 1890, in the foyer of the Drury Lane Theatre, by striking the offending editor Augustus Moore across the face with his cane.

2. Three Whistler lithographs were published in *The Whirlwind:* on 25 October 1890, *The Winged Hat* (w25); on 15 November 1890, *The Tyresmith* (w27); and on 27 December 1890, *Maunder's Fish-shop, Chelsea* (w28). Freer's bound volume of the journal, which ran only from 28 June to 27 December 1890, is in the Rare Books Collection, FGA Library.

3. Thomas Way was the London printer who introduced Whistler to artistic lithography in 1878. Way and his son T. R. Way (1861–1913) printed nearly all of Whistler's lithographs. Freer refers to *Notes,* a portfolio of six lithographs published in 1887; he purchased one set, at four guineas, from the Fine Art Society, London, on 26 March 1888 (FGA Art Vouchers).

4. On 25 October 1888, Freer bought nine lithographs from Wunderlich & Co., New York, for thirty-six dollars (FGA Invoices 1888).

♪ Letter from William Bell to Freer

21 Cheyne Walk,
Chelsea S.W.
June 6 1891.

Dear Sir

I am directed by Mr. Whistler to send off to you the enclosed proof of his first new etching.

He understood that you wished him to select for you anything that he should do.

If you do not wish to keep it will you kindly return it by post in the same flat condition.

The price is £10.10.0. and Mr. Whistler calls it "Cameo No. 1."[1]

Mr. Whistler meant to have written himself but is off to Paris in great haste.

Yours Truly
William Bell
(Private Sec)

FGA Bell 33.

---

1. *Cameo, No. 1* (K347), fig. 20.

Fig. 20. *Cameo, No. 1* (K347), 1891. Etching printed in brown ink on cream-colored laid paper (17.5 x 12.7), 06.108. Inscribed by Whistler, verso, "Selected for Charles L. Freer," and signed with the butterfly.

9 Letter from Beatrix Whistler to Freer

21. Cheyne Walk.
Chelsea.
[29 January 1892]

My dear Mr Freer.

I am sending to you by this mail the Lithographs which you so long ago asked for.[1]

Mr Whistler begs you to forgive him for his long silence. He has been so much occupied, that he has not found a moment for his correspondence, which has grown to enormous dimensions, and which he does not dare face.

He has sent you all the lithographs which are in existence so far, with the exception of the coloured lithographs which are not yet published, in fact, they are the reason of his long silence.

I think when you see them you will think them very beautiful and quite unlike anything of the kind which has been hither to attempted.

The proofs of the lithographs are on Dutch and Japanese paper and are £2-2- a proof. Mr Whistler sends you two sets so that you may show Mr Hecker, in case, he may not have all of them.

You may have some of them already, in which case, will you return those you do not want. Have you heard that Mr Whistlers Mothers

Fig. 21. *Chelsea Rags* (w22), 1888. Lithograph (18.1 x 15.7), 06.148. Probably one of the lithographs Whistler sent to Freer in January 1892.

portrait has been bought by the French Government for the Luxembourg?[2] We are delighted.

Will you give our kindest regards to Mrs and Mr Hecker and Miss Hecker[3]

and with our best wishes for this New Year to you. Believe me

Very sincerely
Beatrix Whistler.

FGA Beatrix Whistler 270. Envelope addressed to Freer at 77 Alfred Street, Detroit; postmarked Chelsea, 29 January 1892, New York, 8 February 1892, and Detroit, 9 February 1892. An American Artist's Declaration for 46 lithographs valued at £96.12.0, signed by Whistler on 16 January 1892, is attached to this letter, although it probably accompanied the package of prints that arrived in February.

---

1. *Chelsea Rags* (w22), fig. 21, was presumably among these. The lithographs Freer probably received in this lot and retained for his collection are listed in appendix B.

2. *Arrangement in Grey and Black: Portrait of the Artist's Mother* was purchased on 27 November 1891 for the Musée du Luxembourg, the national museum for works by living artists of the period, on the instigation of the poet Stéphane Mallarmé (1842–1898) and the art critic Théodore Duret (1838–1927). It was transferred to the Jeu de Paume in 1922, to the Louvre in 1926, and to the Musée d'Orsay in 1987.

3. Probably Anna Hecker (d. 1923), Frank J. Hecker's eldest daughter.

10 Letter from Freer to Beatrix Whistler

77 Alfred St.
Detroit, Mich.
[29 February 1892]

My dear Mrs. Whistler,

Your very kind letter came nearly two weeks ago, but the package of Lithographs was detained at the Custom House until yesterday. At first, the stupid officials who look after our silly revenue affairs here were inclined to issue some ridiculously absurd ruling concerning the pictures, but, in a moment of just indignation, I demanded their clearance in language which I fear was much more blasphemous than courteous, and thereby prevented official utterance of the ruling and got the lithographs. Since then, during calmer moments, I have regretted that I did not allow the foolish ruling to be officially pronounced and published—for while the delight that the possession of the lithographs now gives me would have been deferred, I am sure that I would have been abundantly compensated by the great amusement the proposed edict would have furnished yourself and Mr. Whistler. Should another opportunity of the same kind offer, I shall be more diplomatic.

I cannot tell you how much pleasure I have already gotten from the lithographs and am sure that their charm will continue perpetually. Prior to their arrival my collection contained some fifteen examples of Mr. Whistlers lithographic work, including the "Notes" published by Bussod, Valadon & Co.[1] and a few of the other single figure and outdoor subjects, but in paper, printing and completed beauty they do not approach the lovely impressions you so kindly sent. I wish that your lot might have included the "Nocturne" and "Limehouse" of the Bussod Valadon & Co. set.[2] If fine proofs of these are to be had, wont you please send them along with selected proofs of the coloured lithographs as soon as the latter are ready.

How is Mr. Whistler getting on with his work of retouching the Venice plates? I am told that the new states of the plates are wonderfully beautiful, which I can readily believe.[3] I have been expecting to receive from Mr. Whistler chosen proofs from these retouched plates for my collection and earnestly hope that I wont be disappointed. Will you kindly request Mr. Whistler to send them when he can.

I take much pleasure in enclosing herewith draft on London payable to the order of Mr. Whistler for £98. which I trust will cover the price of the lithographs £96.12 and the expense of the consulate certificate and the express charges both of which were so courteously prepaid—

Accept also my many thanks for your own and Mr. Whistlers kindness.

I was in New York when the word first came to this country, of the well earned honor paid to Mr. Whistler by the French Government. Of course we were very much delighted. This significant recognition of Mr. Whistlers art speaks in many ways and comforts many hearts—and although of universal interest, it is as peculiarily gratifying to all good Americans, as it must be supremely disappointing to the few remaining scalpless followers of Ruskinism.[4]

To Mr. Whistler and yourself I beg to offer my heartiest congratulations.

Mr. and Mrs. Hecker send their kindest regards to yourself and Mr. Whistler and are both much pleased to have the lithographs.

Miss Hecker was married to my youngest brother[5] during November last (a real pleasure to us all) and she also sends her kindest regards. Let me add my own, and also my best wishes, and again, my thanks to yourself and Mr. Whistler.

Faithfully yours
Charles L. Freer
February 29th—1892.

---

1. Boussod, Valadon & Cie. were Paris dealers represented in London by the Goupil Gallery at 116–17 Bond Street.

2. Freer eventually acquired from T. R. Way duplicate impressions of the rare lithotints *Nocturne* (W5), 05.208, and *Limehouse* (W4), 06.60.

3. In 1890 Whistler began working on new states of the Venice etchings, which he had first made in 1879–80. See Katharine A. Lochnan, *The Etchings of James McNeill Whistler* (New Haven: Yale University Press, 1984), 254.

4. An allusion to Whistler's famous and successful lawsuit in 1878 against the eminent English art critic John Ruskin (1819–1900).

5. Watson Freer (1863–1922).

11 Letter from Beatrix Whistler to Freer

33, Rue de Tournon,
Paris
[19 March 1892]

My dear Mr Freer.

Your kind letter has followed us here, where we have been staying for some time.[1]

We are very pleased that you and Mr Hecker like the lithographs. They certainly do look beautiful on the Dutch paper. I think I sent you one or two on Japanese. Which do you like best?

Mr Whistler thanks you very much for the charming things you said about the purchase of his mother's picture by the French Government.

You would be very much amused at the difference it has made in the tone of the London papers!! They say it is disgrace to England, that such a picture was allowed to go out of the country, quite ignoring the fact that this is one of the pictures they laughed at!! Two or three have said "Whistlers" are the only pictures which will gain in value as time goes on! &c &c.

We are very interested in the exhibition of the pictures the Goupils have borrowed, which opens next Monday.[2] It will be curious to see the result.

I hope Mr. Whistler will be able to borrow some for Chicago.[3]

What is this that we see in a Glasgow paper, that there has been some talk in Chicago of commissioning Mr Whistler to paint a picture in commemoration of the Chicago Exhibition as it was his Grandfather who selected the site of the city, which I believe is quite true.[4] Will you let us know if you have heard anything of this? Will you tell Mrs Freer how much we congratulate her on her marriage, or rather how much we congratulate your brother.

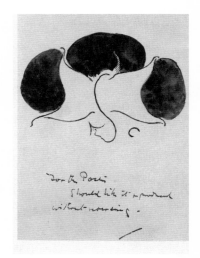

Fig. 22. Butterfly for the poster for "Nocturnes, Marines, & Chevalet Pieces," illustrating a letter from Whistler to T. R. Way, written in Paris, 6 March 1892.

With our kindest regards to you and Mr & Mrs Hecker, Believe me

Very sincerely yours
Beatrix Whistler

P.S. Mr Whistler will select the Venice etchings for you.

FGA Beatrix Whistler 274. Envelope addressed to Freer at Alfred Street, Detroit; postmarked Paris (rue de Vaugirard), 19 March 1892, New York, 28 March 1892, and Detroit, 30 March 1892; with a notation in Freer's hand, "answd."

---

1. In 1892 the Whistlers moved to Paris and lived at the Hôtel Foyot in the rue du Tournon until the summer, when alterations were completed on their house at 110 rue du Bac. Whistler took a studio in the rue Notre Dame des Champs.

2. "Nocturnes, Marines, & Chevalet Pieces," Whistler's retrospective exhibition of forty-three paintings, was organized by Boussod, Valadon & Cie. and held at the Goupil Gallery in London from 21 March to 9 April 1892 (fig. 22).

3. A reference to the World's Columbian Exposition, or World's Fair, that was held in Chicago 1 May through 26 October 1893.

4. The *Glasgow Herald* reported on 19 March (apparently without foundation) that Whistler had received a commission for "The Child of Chelsea," a painting to commemorate the World's Fair: "Grandfather Whistler did not hit on a first-rate position for the City, but the commemorative picture will probably supply deficiencies in the landscape" (GUL Whistler Presscuttings 13:13). Whistler's grandfather Captain John Whistler had initiated the construction in 1803 of Fort Dearborn on the site of the city of Chicago, and his uncle William Whistler served as commander there in 1883. See Arthur Jerome Eddy, *Recollections & Impressions of James A. McNeill Whistler* (Philadelphia: Lippincott, 1903), 26–27. An earlier painting by Whistler called *The Chelsea Girl* (Private collection), then in the possession of Alexander J. Cassatt (1839–1906)—brother of the artist Mary Cassatt—was shown in Chicago. Whistler objected to its exhibition because it was not, he said, "a *representative* finished picture!" (Whistler to Edward G. Kennedy, 21 September 1893, Edward Guthrie Kennedy Papers, New York Public Library).

12   Letter from Freer to Beatrix Whistler

77 Alfred St.
Detroit, Mich.
[6 May 1892]

My dear Mrs. Whistler,

Owing to an absence of several weeks from home, your valued letter of March 19th written at Paris did not reach me until about ten days ago, since then I have visited New York and Chicago and at each place I have made careful inquiry of the persons I met who were likely to know about the commission rumored to be offered to Mr. Whistler to paint a picture to commemorate the Chicago Exhibition &c. but thus far I have failed to learn of any decisive action having been taken. On May 16th, one week from Monday next, a convention of american artists and art lovers is to be held in Washington for the purpose of organizing a National Art Association.[1] The desire being to remove the duty on art, to organize a Government Commission of Art and Architecture and to make true art more accessible to the masses.

This convention promises to be attended by nearly all of the prominent collectors and amateurs of this country.

While at the convention I shall learn all that I can concerning the facts of the talked of commission to Mr. Whistler, and if anything of note is brought out or developed in the matter, I will write you promptly and fully. I heartily wish that such a work might be undertaken by Mr. Whistler for it would stand [as] a lasting monument of the best art of this century—may I add of any century?—commemorating an event of the utmost consequence to the American people and furnishing inspiration in the years to come to countless thousands who are destined to study Art for its real value and enjoy collections of Art in this country second to none in existence.

The coming years will see extraordinary sums of

American money spent for art—The question of the day should be; what steps shall be taken to properly start a movement of such great educational and social importance.

How unfortunate that discrimination in such matters is so rare!

The beautiful lot of Lithographs give me increasing pleasure. I am particularly interested in the single figures, the charming old bridge over the Thames, the interior of the blacksmith shop and the outdoor scene of the tea party, but it is very hard to choose when all are so beautiful.[2]

May I soon expect the colored Lithographs and the Venice etchings?

Is Mr. Whistler doing any work in pastel this spring? I must have another some day to hang beside the extraordinary one I brought home with me two years ago.[3] It is what we americans call "great." Also some day I hope to have another water color—a companion for the Liverpool from the Wunderlich Exhibition[4]—possibly I might be favored with a springtime landscape showing the first flush and delicate tones of early spring the new life, a resurrection thought you know—or perhaps this idea might be beautifully translated in a single figure in pastel—perhaps the same thought for each of the pictures, different of course in treatment as well as medium?

I have read many notices of Mr. Whistlers London Exhibition and am glad to know that it has been genuinely successful in the best way. Can you tell me how to secure a copy of the catalogue?[5]

My sister bids me thank you for your kind remembrance and congratulations—

With kindest regards to yourself and Mr. Whistler, I am

Sincerely yours
Charles L. Freer
May 6/1892

GUL Whistler F436.

1. Accepting membership in the new association, Freer wrote that same day to Kate Field, its representative, "The result you hope to achieve, if attained, will be of great value to the American people" (FGA Letterpress Book 1).

2. Freer probably refers to *Old Battersea Bridge* (w12), 88.27, *The Farriers* (w24), 06.150, and *The Garden* (w38), fig. 19. See appendix B.

3. *Harmony in Blue and Violet*, plate 6.

4. *Grey and Silver: The Mersey*, 89.3, which Freer purchased as "Grey & Silver —Liverpool" on 3 May 1889 from Wunderlich & Co., New York, after the major exhibition in March of Whistler's works, "'Notes'—'Harmonies'—'Nocturnes.'"

5. Whistler designed the exhibition catalogue *Nocturnes, Marines, & Chevalet Pieces,* published in London by the Goupil Gallery, which contained extracts from previous reviews. Freer eventually obtained three copies, now in the Rare Books Collection, FGA Library.

13 Telegram from Freer to Whistler

DETROIT
[28 November 1892]

AS OWNER YOUR PAINTING THE BALCONY HAVE CONSENTED TO EXHIBIT RETROSPECTIVE EXHIBITION SOCIETY AMERICAN ARTISTES[1] HARPER BROTHERS WISH TO REPRODUCE PAINTING[2] CABLE YOUR WISHES.

C. L. FREER

GUL Whistler F437 (typescript copy, FGA Letterpress Book 1). Delivered to Whistler at 110 rue du Bac, Paris; stamped Paris (Bourse), 28 November 1892.

1. Society of American Artists, Fifth Avenue Art Galleries, New York, 5–25 December 1892. Freer purchased *Variations in Flesh Colour and Green: The Balcony,* plate 1, from Wunderlich & Co., New York, on 27 September 1892.

2. The painting was published in John C. Van Dyke, "Retrospective Exhibition of the Society of American Artists," *Harper's Weekly* 36 (17 December 1892), 1212.

14 Letter from Freer to Whistler

33 Ferry Avenue.
Detroit, Michigan.
January 9th 1894.

My dear Mr. Whistler,

This will doubtless seem to you a very late hour for me to mention the World's Fair of 1893. But accepting the old adage of better late than never I now want to thank you for the very great pleasure I received from your paintings and etchings then shown—The Yellow Buskin, The Fur Jacket and Nocturne, Valparaiso seemed supremely fine.[1] Of the etchings and dry points and their selection, arrangement and location too much favorably cannot be said.

Your work of course completely overshadowed everything in the Fine Arts Department, and gave pleasure and inspiration to many more people than you imagine. The management was extremely anxious to have me send The Balcony[2] and I wish now that I had done so. But at the time pictures were being gathered together for the Fair, The Balcony had just returned from the opening exhibition of the new building of the Society of American Artists, where the wood panel had checked considerably, and I was afraid of similar danger—dampness—in the building at Chicago. Time proved however, that the fine arts building at Chicago was perfectly safe. I had nine other paintings there besides some prints and all were returned unharmed. I was happy to receive from you, through Mr. Kennedy, the charming little proof

Fig. 23. After Whistler's *Variations in Flesh Colour and Green: The Balcony.* Wood engraving (15.6 x 12.1), 98.243. Inscribed on the mat, "premier etat." Wunderlich & Co., New York, sent the engraving to Freer as a "presentation from Mr. Whistler" on 16 September 1893.

of the engraving of The Balcony: accept please my best thanks.[3]

What shall I say concerning the delightful set of photographs of your paintings which you have caused to be issued?[4] And also those wonderful lithographs recently received. Well, I presume so much has already been said in their praise that further comments coming from me might seem to you presumptuous, so I will simply say thank you, for the delight they have given my friends and myself.

When am I to have impressions from your retouched Venetian plates and the new French plates on which I hear you have been recently working.[5] You are reserving selected impressions from all of these plates for me, I trust.

As I told you in London I have so much trouble to get satisfactory proofs from the dealers, I would greatly prefer to purchase direct from you, and you can depend upon my taking at least one impression of each of your etchings, dry points and lithographs. Will it trouble you too much to select and forward to me accordingly?

Life, in Paris, I hope proves very agreeable to both Mrs. Whistler and yourself and you are both enjoying good health, I trust.

With cordial greetings,

Faithfully yours,
Charles L. Freer

James McNeil Whistler, Esq.
Paris.

P.S. Please note change of address to my new residence 33 Ferry Avenue, instead of the old 77 Alfred St. C.L.F.

GUL Whistler F438. Personal stationery.

---

1. Whistler was represented in the American section of the Department of Fine Arts by a selection of etchings and six paintings, including *Arrangement in Black: La Dame au brodequin jaune—Portrait of Lady Archibald Campbell* (Philadelphia Museum of Art), *Arrangement in Black and Brown: The Fur Jacket* (Worcester Art Museum, Massachusetts), and *Nocturne: Blue and Gold—Valparaiso,* which later entered Freer's collection (09.127).

2. *Variations in Flesh Colour and Green: The Balcony,* plate 1.

3. Edward Guthrie Kennedy (1849–1932), a partner in Wunderlich & Co., represented Whistler in New York after 1885. Kennedy's definitive catalogue of Whistler's etchings was published in 1910 by the Grolier Club. The engraving Freer mentions is shown in fig. 23.

4. *Nocturnes—Marines—Chevalet Pieces,* a portfolio of twenty-four photographs of Whistler's paintings published after the Goupil Gallery exhibition. Freer purchased his album, one of one hundred with photographs signed by the artist, on 4 August 1893, and annotated each picture; it is now in the Rare Books Collection, FGA Library.

5. In 1892 and 1893, Whistler etched twenty-three Parisian scenes; Freer purchased several of the etchings from Whistler's Company of the Butterfly sometime after 1897. See Katharine A. Lochnan, *The Etchings of James McNeill Whistler* (New Haven: Yale University Press, 1984), 260–64.

15 Letter from Whistler to Freer

110. Rue du Bac.
Paris
[18 July 1894]

Dear Mr. Freer. I have always meant to write to you in answer to your letter, received some time ago. How is it that you do not turn up here?

Certainly one might have expected to see you in Paris before now!

You will be pleased I fancy to hear that I have been doing some new lithographs lately—and am at once sending you the proofs as you asked me to—

I shall send two of each while I am about it, as I did once before I think, so that your friend Mr. Hecker can have his lot too—

Now you said in one of your letters that you would like me to do you a figure —to, in a way, hint at "Spring"[1]—

How would you like this? I mean shall it be a painting in oil?—and shall it be a sort of cabinet size?—

Well I daresay I shall manage some thing charming—

I have half a mind to send you, meanwhile, a very

Fig. 24. *La Belle Jardinière* (w63), 1894. Lithograph (22.5 x 15.9), 06.180. Beatrix Whistler in the garden of 110 rue du Bac. Freer bought this lithograph from Whistler in November 1894.

{92}

pretty pastel—I don't remember quite, but I think you have one—However I have been doing some lately that I am sure you would be delighted with.

When are you again coming abroad?

Of course we shall expect to see you here.

With kindest regards

Very sincerely Yours
J. McN. Whistler

FGA Whistler 35. Envelope addressed to Freer at 33 Ferry Avenue, Detroit; postmarked Paris (rue du Bac), 18 July 1894, and Detroit, 30 July 1894.

---

1. See letter 12.

16 Letter from Freer to Whistler

33 Ferry Avenue.
[Detroit]
[2 August 1894]

Dear Mr. Whistler;

I was much pleased to receive your recent letter, which came yesterday.

Let me thank you for the kindly remembrance and all that your letter contained. My visit to your Tite St. studio and the kindness of yourself and Mrs. Whistler gave me lasting pleasure.

In about six weeks I shall leave America for a year's vacation; taking the Mediterranean route—Venice during October, Paris probably during November. After which, a tinge of Hollands winter, then India, and, if war does not prevent, Japan and home via San Francisco.

While in Paris I hope to see you and shall surely look you up. I am delighted to know that you have been doing some new pastels and lithographs and that you have kindly forwarded two each of the latter for my friend Mr. Hecker and myself.

My collection of your work in lithography is a source of genuine delight to such of my visitors as I feel confident you would care to please. As for myself: it is hard to choose between the etchings, dry-points, lithographs, pastels and "The Balcony."[1]

Yes, I am fortunate enough to possess three of your pastels—two single figures and a marvellous sketch of Venice from the sea at early evening.[2] I trust you did finally conclude to send me the pastel mentioned in your letter. If not already shipped, why not start it so that it will reach me before Sept. 15th?

I hope you will do that figure about which I wrote you—to, in a way, hint at spring.[3]

Let the medium suit your own taste and mood. It will of course be charming. If pastel, what would you say to making it about 8 x 12? If oil, would 16 x 20 please you and would one, so important, be within my financial reach? Some day I must have one of your marine nocturnes also. How beautiful the one brought over during the early summer for Mr. Johnson of Philadelphia![4]

With kindest regards to yourself and Mrs. Whistler,

Very sincerely yours,
Charles L. Freer.
Detroit, Mich.
August 2, 1894.

<hr>

1. *Variations in Flesh Colour and Green: The Balcony,* plate 1.

2. Freer purchased *Harmony in Blue and Violet,* plate 6, from Whistler in March 1890 and *The Blue Dress,* 92.24, a study for Whistler's portrait of Mrs. Frederick R. Leyland, from Wunderlich & Co., New York, on 27 September 1892. A year later, on 16 September, he purchased *Venice,* 93.26, from the same dealer.

3. See letter 12.

4. John G. Johnson (1841–1917), a Philadelphia attorney and art collector, had purchased *Nocturne: Grey and Silver* (Philadelphia Museum of Art, John G. Johnson Collection).

17 Letter from Whistler to Freer

110. Rue du Bac.
Paris.
Aug. 8. 1894

Dear Mr. Freer—I am sending you today by post twenty two proofs of my later lithographs, as I told you I would do, when I last wrote to you.[1]

I hope you will be pleased with them—as they are on beautiful old Dutch & Japanese paper.

There are two sets, as I supposed that your friend Mr Hecker might wish to have one also.

The enclosed list corresponds in numbers with the numbers you find in pencil on the backs of proofs—

Do write me directly you receive the proofs as I shall be anxious to know that they arrive safely and in perfect condition.

With kindest regards

Very sincerely
J McN Whistler

[enclosure]

Lithographs

			proofs	
No.	1.	"The Novel—draped figure"	2	£4-4
"	2.	The seated figure (3 gs each)	2	6-6
"	3.	Draped figure, back view	2	4-4
"	4.	Nude figure—lying down	2	4-4
"	5.	The long Balcony	2	4-4
		(Paris windows during Carnots funeral)		
"	6.	The little Balcony	2	4-4
"	7.	The Tête a Tête, Garden	2	4-4
"	8.	The Long Gallery, Louvre[2]	2	4-4
"	9.	The Terrace Luxembourg	2	4-4
"	10.	The Draped figure, leaning	2	4-4
"	11.	Le Rétameur de l'Impasse	2	4-4

£48-6

To Charles L. Freer. Esq.
Detroit Michigan
Aug. 8. 1894

Fig. 25. *The Long Gallery, Louvre* (w52), 1894. Lithograph (21.6 x 15.6), 06.168.

FGA Whistler 36. Envelope addressed to Freer at 33 Ferry Avenue, Detroit; postmarked Paris, 8 August 1894, and Detroit, 19 August 1894. Receipt confirming that Whistler had received a check from Freer in the amount of £48.6.0 ($235.82) on 23 August 1894 is attached.

---

1. The impressions Freer received are listed in appendix B.

2. *The Long Gallery, Louvre* (w52), fig. 25.

18 Whistler's calling card, inscribed to Freer

[Paris]
[probably 14
November 1894]

Dear Mr Freer—Delighted. I shall appear at the hotel a little before eight on Saturday[1]—

But also I am told by McMonnies who is here at this moment, that I am to have the pleasure of seeing you & Mr Dewing tomorrow evening at 8[2]—

FGA Whistler 43-f. Card imprinted, "Mr. J. McNeill Whistler, / Cheyne Walk, Chelsea. / 110, Rue du Bac." Inscription in pencil on verso. Probably delivered in unstamped envelope (FGA Whistler 43) addressed to Freer at Hotel Windsor (rue de Rivoli, Paris).

---

1. According to Freer's pocket diary, he had dinner with Whistler on Saturday, 17 November, after meeting with French sculptor Auguste Rodin (1840–1917) in the afternoon.

2. Frederick William MacMonnies (1863–1937) was an American sculptor residing in Paris; his *Triumph of Columbia* had been commissioned for the 1893 World's Fair. Thomas Wilmer Dewing (1851–1938), an American figure painter and friend of Freer's who was living temporarily in London, came to Paris on 11 November, the day after Freer arrived. The dinner Whistler refers to was probably one Freer gave in Whistler's honor on 15 November.

19 Whistler's calling card, inscribed to Freer

[Paris]
[possibly 17
November 1894]

Dear Mr Freer, then, à ce soir & I am delighted![1]—Many
thanks for the really extraordinary engraving[2]—

FGA Whistler 43-d. Card imprinted, "Mr. J. McNeill Whistler, / Cheyne Walk,
Chelsea. / 110, Rue du Bac." Probably delivered in unstamped envelope (FGA
Whistler 43) addressed to Freer at Hotel Windsor, rue de Rivoli (Paris).

---

1. Freer's pocket diary shows that he dined with Whistler on 15, 17, and 22
November.

2. Wood engraving made in 1892–94 by American artist Elbridge Kingsley
(1842–1918) after *Springtime,* 93.14, painted in 1892 by Dwight William Tryon
(1849–1925), an American artist who was a close friend of Freer's and whose
work Freer collected. Freer wrote Tryon of Whistler's delight in the print: "I
took him the impression you selected and marked for him. He bid me thank
both yourself and Kingsley. The technical qualities of the printing, engraving
and of course, the whole thing in fact, rather puzzled him. He declared it
refreshing and modern and charming" (typescript copy, 9 December 1894,
Nelson C. White Papers, Archives of American Art, Smithsonian Institution).

20 Whistler's account, endorsed by Freer

[Paris]
[16–17 November 1894][1]

		proofs	gs.
1.	La Blanchisseuse de la Place Dauphine	2	8
2.	"The Lady sleeps"[2]	2	10
3.	La belle dame paresseuse	2	8
4.	The new draped figure	2	6
5.	Confidences dans le jardin[3]	2	6
6.	The president [?] Dr Whistler	2	8
7.	The pas [illegible]	2	6
8.	The little café au bois	2	6
9.	Les Bébés du Luxembourg	2	4
10.	The Smith of the passage[4]	2	6
11.	The Forge of the passage du Dragon	2	6
12.	Le robe rouge	2	8
13.	The Sisters	2	8
14.	La Fruitière de la rue de Grenelle	2	8
15.	Le Rue de Furstenburg	2	6
16.	La Belle Jardinière[5]	2	8
17.	La jolie New Yorkaise, Louis Quinze	2	8
18.	The late Picquet	2	6
19.	The porch[6]	1	2
20.	New draped figure back view (with chair)	2	6
No. 3.	La belle dame paresseuse	1	4

138

[in Freer's hand]
138£
  6.18 20/138
_____

£144.18 6.18
_____

Dear Mr Whistler,

I take much pleasure in handing you endorsed herein draft on London for the above acct.

C. L. Freer
11/17/94

Account in Whistler's hand, FGA Art Inventories (Whistler/Miscellaneous); copy in another hand, with Freer's endorsement, GUL Whistler F440.

---

1. The impressions Freer acquired are listed in appendix B. Freer wrote to Hecker, for whom the duplicate lithographs were intended, that the impressions he had purchased were "all superb. Some of them are the very first and just from the printer and are not in the Wunderlich Exhibition," by which he meant a show of forty lithographs that had opened in New York that October (16 November 1894, FGA Hecker).

2. *La Belle Dame Endormie* (w69), fig. 4.

3. A different impression of *Confidences in the Garden* (w60) is shown in fig. 6.

4. *The Smith. Passage du Dragon* (w73), fig. 26.

5. *La Belle Jardinière* (w63), fig. 24.

6. Freer explained to Hecker that there was only one impression of "The Porch," or *The Garden Porch* (w140), 06.198, because Whistler considered it "very bad and fit only as collectors proof which I am to return to him later in exchange for another should the stone eventually give satisfactory proofs" (16 November 1894, FGA Hecker). Only eight impressions of the lithograph were ever printed.

Fig. 26. *The Smith. Passage du Dragon* (w73), 1894. Lithograph (24.5 x 15.7), 06.187.

21 Whistler's receipt, sent to Freer

110 Rue du Bac,
Paris
17. Nov. 1894.

Received from Mr Charles L. Freer
cheque £144.18—for proofs—Lithographs—

J McNeill Whistler

FGA Whistler 268.

22 Letter from Freer to Whistler

[Hotel Windsor,
rue de Rivoli]
Paris.
Nov. 23rd [1894]

Dear Mr. Whistler;

Let me thank you most heartily for your many kind-nesses to Mr. Dewing and myself—also permit me the pleasure of handing you enclosed herewith draft on London for 1300 gs. for the pictures.

Should I not return via Paris, kindly send the "Blue Girl" to me at Detroit, after the Salon closes.[1] The water color and two pastels might go at the same time or earlier if you wish.[2]

In my absence from Detroit my friend Mr. Frank J. Hecker attends to my personal affairs.

The pictures will give me great delight and America is most fortunate to possess them—

Faithfully
Charles L. Freer

My Detroit address is
33 Ferry Avenue.
Indian address,
c/o Thos. Cook & Sons
Bombay.

GUL Whistler F441.

---

1. Whistler apparently planned to show the commissioned painting, *Harmony in Blue and Gold: The Little Blue Girl*, plate 2, the following spring at the exhibition of the Société Nationale des Beaux-Arts in the Champs de Mars, a rival to the *Salon ancien*. He did not exhibit at the Paris Salon after becoming a founding *sociétaire* in 1891.

2. The watercolor painting is *Blue and Gold—The Rose Azalea*, plate 8. The pastel drawings are *A Violet Note—Spring*, plate 4, and *Rose and Red: The Little Pink Cap*, plate 9.

23 Letter from Whistler to Freer

[110 rue du Bac]
[Paris]
[23 November 1894]

My dear Mr Freer—I am delighted as I told you to know that my little Blue Girl[1] is to be always in your care!—

You have written me a kind and charming letter and in this hurried line I do not pretend to tell you how delightful your visit has been to me, and how really sorry I am to say

Good bye—We all however rely upon your return in the Spring—and will never forgive Mansfield if he carry you off in spite of of [sic] our superior fascinations!

I like Dewing too very much, and shall miss you both—yesterday afternoon is not readily forgotten in the studio!

My wife is so glad that she saw you yesterday before your going off—& now she bids me say that you are not to trouble yourself terribly with the bird if he turns out to be bigger than we fancied!—

We both or rather all of us wish you the best of bon voyages, and great luck!—

Always yours sincerely
J McN Whistler

110. Rue du Bac. Paris.
23. Nov. 1894

Received from Mr. Charles L. Freer, cheque for Thirteen Thousand guineas[2] for the following works—
"Harmony in Blue & Gold—The little Blue Girl"
oil painting
and three drawings in pastel & water colour.[3]

J. McNeill Whistler

FGA Whistler 37 (copy, GUL Whistler LB4:31–32; typescript, GUL Whistler F442); butterfly signature in margin of letter. Unstamped envelope addressed to Freer at Hotel Windsor, rue de Rivoli (Paris).

---

1. *Harmony in Blue and Gold: The Little Blue Girl*, plate 2.

2. Freer paid Whistler thirteen *hundred* guineas (see letter 22).

3. The "drawings" are the pastels *A Violet Note—Spring*, plate 4, and *Rose and Red: The Little Pink Cap*, plate 9, and the watercolor *Blue and Gold—The Rose Azalea*, plate 8.

24 Letter from Frank J. Hecker to Whistler

> Michigan-Peninsular
> Car Company.
> Detroit,
> Dec. 20, 1894.

My dear Mr. Whistler:

Owing either to the stupidity or bull-headedness on the part of the customs officers here, I am having difficulty in clearing the 39 lithographs Mr. Freer shipped from Paris.[1] They want a consular certificate that the 39 lithographs are your work and that you are an American artist. Failing this they will require duty to be paid on them and pending receipt of a reply from you I have given bond. Can you without too great inconvenience obtain such a certificate from our consul and forward to me at your early convenience.

My latest advices from Mr. Freer are from Colombo by cable and a letter from Alexandria. He had a pleasant passage and reports being in the best of health.

With personal regards to yourself and asking for kindly remembrance to Mrs. Whistler and with the compliments of the season,

> Sincerely yours,
> Frank J Hecker

Mr. J. McNeil Whistler,
110 Rue Du Bac,
Paris, France.

GUL Whistler H167. Company letterhead.

---

1. See letter 20.

25 Letter from Freer to Beatrix Whistler

Calcutta,
March 18, 1895.

My dear Mrs. Whistler;

Tomorrow is to be my last day in India for on the day following I start for Japan. This afternoon, I started a final hunt for a Shama Merle[1] for you and succeeded in finding the long looked for bird. Nothing could have been more fortunate than my afternoon experience. During my travels all over India, I constantly searched for the songster, but found him only in museums, stuffed. While in Calcutta, ten days ago, I searched the native quarters fruitlessly and was told my only chance of getting one would be at Darjeeling, in the Himalayan mountains. But, no! not one had ever been sold there, so far as I could find out.

This morning, I received a suggestion which took me to an out of the way place in the suburbs of this city, where I finally, this afternoon, found three splendid specimens of the Shama Merle for sale, and what was equally important under the circumstances, a reputable dealer, and Capt. Doherr of the steamer Baroda of the Hamburg Calcutta Line. Capt. Doherr is a great bird and animal lover, and buys rare species for European collections, also for Mr. Hagenbeck of world-wide animal fame.[2] The Capt. had purchased from the dealer a number of animals, several dozen birds of various kinds, and had partially bargained for two of the Merles when I arrived. He had also just engaged the services of a native expert to accompany him to Hamburg to care for his purchases. Capt. Doherr is a true gentleman and after learning that I wanted a pair of the Merles for you he not only released the two for which he had partially bargained but also volunteered to deliver the birds to you in Paris.

Now, what do you think of that for luck?

The dealer, Mr. Rutledge, a Hindu, not to be out done, said he would secure a fourth merle before the Baroda sailed, so that both the Capt. and you could have two each. As the Capt. would not accept any pay for taking the birds forward, I insisted upon paying the purchase price of the four (a mere trifle) to which the Capt. finally assented with the understanding that in case of the death of any of the merles he should have the right to send you the choice of whatever number survived.

As Capt. Doherr has no personal arrangements for taking birds beyond Hamburg he said that he would tell Mr. Hagenbeck that the birds are for you and with such information Mr. Hagenbeck would be delighted to forward [them] from Hamburg to Paris—How beautiful, courteous and gentlemanly!!

This is not half as bad a world as some would have us believe.

I am charmed over my days experience. It does me good to meet such men!! And I am happy to have secured the birds you desire. They are beauties and real songsters. I do hope they will reach you safely and trust that they will give many, many hours of enjoyment.

I have thought of you often since leaving Paris and have wished much for your return to health—you are stronger, I hope, and your complete recovery is not far distant I trust.

And Mr. Whistler remains perfectly well, I hope. He was so kind to my friend Mr. Dewing and myself while we were in your city.

My stay in India has brought me much happiness and I am already counting on another trip to this country of wonders.

Next Japan!!!

Good bye, and may the best of all things be yours,

Very sincerely
Charles L. Freer.

Care of Hong Kong and Shanghai Bank
Yokohama, Japan

P.S. Pardon this long letter, but I wanted you to know of Capt. Doherr's kindness.

GUL Whistler F443.

---

1. A songbird native to China and Southeast Asia.

2. Karl Hagenbeck (1844–1913), German animal trainer and circus director who toured Europe and the United States after 1866 and established near Hamburg in 1907 the first open-air zoo.

26 Letter from Freer to Whistler

33 Ferry Avenue.
[Detroit]
September 23rd, 1895.

My dear Mr. Whistler;

After leaving India I continued my travels Eastward, by easy stages, stopping four months in bewitching Japan, and finally reached home a few days ago in perfect health and charmed with the experiences of my trip. Your kindness to me during my stay in Paris is one of my most delightful memories.

How are you all? Mrs. Whistler has quite recovered her health, I trust. I thought of her often during my journeying and if good wishes count her illness must have long since departed. Are you nearly ready to make us a visit? I hope so.

And The "Little Blue Girl" and the three drawings in pastel and water colour, are they soon to come to me?[1]

Detroit is a port of entry and they can be shipped direct to my house address. The safer way would be in care of American Express Co. from New York city. Please let transportation and any other charges including American consular certificate follow.

  With warmest personal regards to you all.

Most faithfully yours,
Charles L. Freer

Detroit.
Michigan
U.S.A.

When you see MacMonies [MacMonnies] kindly give him my cordial greetings.

C.L.F.

GUL Whistler F444. Personal stationery.

---

1. Freer refers to *Harmony in Blue and Gold: The Little Blue Girl,* plate 2, as well as the pastels *A Violet Note—Spring,* plate 4, and *Rose and Red: The Little Pink Cap,* plate 9, and the watercolor *Blue and Gold: The Rose Azalea,* plate 8.

4, Whitehall Court. S.W.[1]
[London]
Nov. 28–1896[2]

2. The Little Steps—	6 guineas	No. 1
Lyme Regis		
2. The Managers Window,	6—	No. 2
Gaiety Theatre		
2. The Lyme Regis fair	6—	No. 3
2. Sunday—Lyme Regis	6—	No. 4
2. The Priest's House—Rouen	8—	No. 5
2. The Brothers—Lyme Regis	8—	No. 6
1. "Mother & Child (No. 2)"	3—	No. 7
2. The Master Smith—	6—	No. 8
Lyme Regis		
2. Little Dorothy	8—	No. 9
2. Girl with bowl	6—	No. 10
2. The Bonfire—	6—	No. 11
5th November Lyme Regis		
2. The Good Shoe—Lyme Regis	6—	No. 12
2. Fire light, Joseph Pennell	6—	No. 13
2. Fire light, Joseph Pennell	6̶–8	No. 14
2. Mephisto Smith—Lyme Regis	6—	No. 15
2. Mother & Child (No. 1.)	6—	No. 16
2. The Russian Schube	6—	No. 17
2. The Old Smiths Story—	8—	No. 18
Lyme Regis		
2. The Strong Arm, Lyme Regis	6—	No. 19
2. London, from Savoy—	10—	No. 20
St. Pauls[3]		
2. Waterloo bridge from Savoy	10—	No. 21
2. The new Model	6—	No. 22
2. Charing Cross bridge,	10—	No. 23
from Savoy		

1. Little Waterloo—Evening	4—	No. 24
2. The Little doorway— Lyme Regis	8—	No. 25
1. The Little steps— Lyme Regis	3—	No. 26
2. The Smiths Yard— Lyme Regis	10—	No. 27
2. The Butchers dog—Soho	10—	No. 28

53

£201-12-0

[in another hand]
985.32[4]
488 ¾[5]

Fig. 27. *Little London* (w121), 1896. Lithograph (18.7 x 13.6), 96.79. The eastward view from the top of the Savoy Hotel, where the Whistlers stayed during Beatrix's illness.

FGA Art Inventories, Whistler/Miscellaneous (also typescript copy). William Heinemann's personal stationery.

1. After his wife's death on 10 May 1896, Whistler lived with his friend the publisher William Heinemann (1863–1920) at Whitehall Court. Their association had begun with the publication of *The Gentle Art* in 1890, the year Heinemann founded his firm.

2. The impressions Freer acquired are listed in appendix B.

3. *Little London* (w121), fig. 27.

4. The total in dollars. Calculations on the facing page, apparently in Freer's hand, indicate that Frank J. Hecker paid $467 for his share of the lithographs and Freer paid $518.32 for his, which included the three single lithographs (nos. 7, 24, and 26).

5. The meaning of this figure is not known.

28 Letter from Freer to Whistler

33 Ferry Avenue.
Detroit, Michigan
[24 December 1896]

My dear Mr. Whistler;

For all that you sent me in care of Mr. Plumb and for your personal courtesy to him accept please my heartiest appreciation.[1]

The water color and the pastel are even finer, much finer, than when I saw them first in your Paris studio and instantly lost my heart.[2]

And now comes the long wished for Nocturne, and of exactly the kind I most admire—real night, actual nature, unceasing mystery.[3] And to complete my happiness the group of marvellous lithographs, and the portrait and the catalogue with inscriptions most charming and friendly.[4] Mr. Hecker begs your acceptance of his thanks for the duplicate lithographs sent.

Accept please for our joint account the draft herewith for £201-12 as per memoranda received.[5]

And, now, I beg you to let me know by return mail how much I may be permitted to remit you in payment for the beautiful Nocturne—a great treasure!!

Are you not coming to America soon?

Try it for awhile and give us an opportunity to shake your hand again.

Again thanking you most sincerely for your great kindness, believe me, my dear Mr. Whistler,

most cordially yours
Charles L. Freer.

J. McNeill Whistler, Esq.

GUL Whistler F466. Personal stationery. Notation in another hand, "From
CHARLES L. FREER (?1890)."

---

1. R. E. Plumb, a business associate of Freer's, was in London and Paris during
the autumn of 1896, and Freer provided him with a letter of introduction to
Whistler in hopes that he would be able to obtain Freer's long-awaited
works. By 14 November, Plumb had met Whistler and reported to Freer that
although the painting would probably not be finished, some etchings (by
which he must have meant lithographs) were ready. See Freer to Plumb, 16
October 1896 and 14 November 1896, FGA Letterpress Books 3 and 4.

2. Freer received the watercolor *Blue and Gold—The Rose Azalea,* plate 8,
and the pastel *Rose and Red: The Little Pink Cap,* plate 9.

3. Whistler had not been able to find a buyer for *Nocturne in Black and Gold:
Entrance to Southampton Water,* plate
10, which is exceptionally dark, even
for a Nocturne. After Freer bought it
in 1897, the tonality continued to
darken and its subject, a boat heading
toward a harbor, has now become
almost illegible. The lantern on the
mast, according to a note attributed
to Freer in the Freer Gallery object
file, was meant to represent Whistler's
butterfly signature.

4. The lithographs are listed in letter
27. The portrait (possibly a photograph) and catalogue have not been
identified.

5. Freer's voucher for $518.32, his
share of the bill for the lithographs, is
addressed to Whistler at 4 Whitehall
Court and dated 24 December 1896
(FGA Art Vouchers).

Fig. 28. T. R. Way (1861–1913), *Portrait of Whistler,* ca. 1895. Lithograph
(9.7 x 7.0), 02.246. Based upon a photograph of the artist in his
garden at 110 rue du Bac, this lithograph served as the frontispiece
to Way's catalogue, *Mr. Whistler's Lithographs,* originally published
in 1896. Way noted in the margin that Whistler himself had altered
the portrait: this version, he wrote, was the "2nd and final state as
used in Catalogue. The difference between the 1st and 2nd state is
entirely due to Mr. Whistler's work on the stone."

[London]
[24 (?) March 1897]

Shall I begin by saying to you, my dear Mr Freer, that your little "Blue & Gold Girl" is doing her very best to look lovely for you?[1]—Perhaps it were well—and so you shall be assured that though steamer after steamer leave me in apparently ungracious silence, it is that only of the pen!

I write to you many letters on your canvas!—and one of these days, you will, by degrees, read them all, as you sit before your picture—

And, in them, you will find, I hope, dimly conveyed, my warm feeling of affectionate appreciation for the friendship that has shown itself to me, in my forlorn destruction—as it had done before, in our happiness, to both of us—And in the work, perhaps, will you, of your refined sympathy and perception, discover the pleasure and interest taken in the perfecting of it, by the other one who, with me, liked you, and delighted in the kind and courteous attention paid, on your travels, to her pretty fancy and expressed wish—

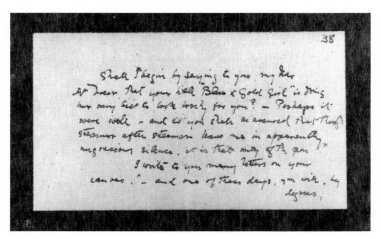

Fig. 29. First page of letter 29, from Whistler to Freer.

Fig. 30. *By the Balcony* (w124), 1895. Lithograph (21.6 x 14.0), 05.212. A rare lithographic portrait of Beatrix Whistler, ill in London, that Freer purchased from Wunderlich & Co., New York, in 1905.

She loved the wonderful bird you sent with such happy care from the distant land!

And when she went—alone, because I was unfit to go too—the strange wild dainty creature stood uplifted on the topmost perch, and sang and sang—as it had never sung before!—A song of the Sun—and of joy—and of my despair!—Loud and ringing clear from the skies! and louder! Peal after peal, until it became a marvel the tiny beast, torn by such glorious voice, should live!—

And suddenly it was made known to me that in this mysterious magpie waif from beyond the temples of India, the spirit of my beautiful Lady had lingered on its way—and the song was her song of love—and courage—and command that the work, in which she had taken her part, should be complete—and so was her farewell!—

I have kept her house—in its freshness and rare beauty—as she had made it—and from time to time, I go to miss her in it—

And, in my wanderings, I may come—who knows? to you—as we both had meant to do!

J McNeill Whistler

FGA Whistler 38 (autograph copy and typescript, GUL Whistler F445; copy, GUL Whistler LB4:25–26). Mourning stationery. Envelope addressed to Freer at 33 Ferry Avenue, Detroit; sealed with black wax imprinted with butterfly stamp; postmarked (place illegible) 24 (?) March 1897, and New York, 1 April (1897), and Syracuse, 2 April 1897; with notation, verso, in Freer's hand, "Very important letter." Published in Agnes E. Meyer, *Charles Lang Freer and His Gallery* (Washington, D.C.: Freer Gallery of Art, 1970), 7–8; and Nigel Thorp, ed., *Whistler on Art: Selected Letters and Writings of James McNeill Whistler* (Washington, D.C.: Smithsonian Institution Press, 1994), 152–53.

---

1. *Harmony in Blue and Gold: The Little Blue Girl*, plate 2.

30 Cablegram from Freer to Whistler

[Detroit]
MARCH 31/97

KINDLY ADVISE WHAT AMOUNT TO SEND YOU FOR "NOCTURNE" RECEIVED. CAN YOU FORWARD "BLUE GIRL" AND PASTEL[1] TO REACH ME BEFORE APRIL FIFTEENTH AND SAVE ME TWENTY FIVE PER CENT. DUTY?
FREER
CHG. C. L. FREER.
2:35

Typescript copy, FGA Letterpress Book 4. Sent to Whistler at his studio address, 8 Fitzroy Street, London.

---

1. Freer had received *Nocturne in Black and Gold: Entrance to Southampton Water,* plate 10. He still awaited *Harmony in Blue and Gold: The Little Blue Girl,* plate 2, and the pastel *A Violet Note—Spring,* plate 4.

31 Cablegram from Freer to Whistler

[Detroit]
APRIL 6, 1897

YOUR LETTER RECEIVED TO-DAY. REGRET LAST WEEK'S CABLE.
LET NOTHING DISTURB YOU. WHEN THE WORK[1] IS DONE TO
YOUR SATISFACTION, WE SHALL HOPE FOR THE ARRIVAL OF
YOU AND IT TOGETHER.
FREER
CH.G C. L. FREER.
4:35

Typescript copy, FGA Letterpress Book 4. Sent to Whistler at 8 Fitzroy Street,
London.

---

1. *Harmony in Blue and Gold: The Little Blue Girl*, plate 2.

32 Letter from Freer to Whistler

33 Ferry Avenue.
[Detroit]
[6 April 1897]

My dear Mr. Whistler;

Your letter with its exquisite memories, tenderness and
friendship came this morning, and as I read of <u>her</u> sympathetic
interest in the "Little Blue and Gold Girl" and realized for
her sake, how precious its care and deeply loving each
finishing touch, my heart sank at the thought of having

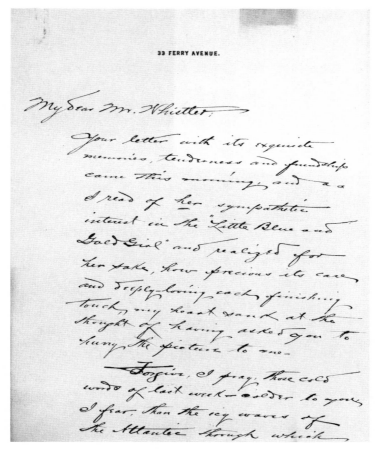

33 FERRY AVENUE.

Fig. 31. First page of letter 32, from Freer to Whistler.

asked you to hurry the picture to me.[1]

　　Forgive, I pray, those cold words of last week[2]—colder to you, I fear, than the icy waves of the Atlantic through which they were flashed. And be assured, my dear Mr. Whistler, that whenever, in your own good time and way, you are quite ready to complete, and transfer to my keeping, that which she loved, and which all who have seen loves, I shall be rejoiced to receive, and care for as you would have me. And when I am gone, the picture shall rest with its own beautiful kind, so, "that in after years, others shall pass that way, and understand."[3]

May and June are our pleasantest months, and then, if you come to us, as we hope you will, the flow of the sea, and of travel will favor your voyage, and you will find warmth, and sympathy, and appreciation everywhere.

Charles L. Freer.

GUL Whistler F446. Personal stationery.

1. *Harmony in Blue and Gold: The Little Blue Girl,* plate 2.

2. See letter 30.

3. The source of this quotation has not been identified.

𝓙𝓙 Cablegram from Whistler to Freer

LONDON 302 PM
[14 July 1897]

FREER
DETROIT (MICH).
SOUTHAMPTON 600.[1] WILL WRITE.
WHISTLER

FGA Whistler 34. Western Union Telegraph Company cable message. Received in Detroit on 14 July 1897.

1. Whistler gives the price in British sterling of *Nocturne in Black and Gold: Entrance to Southampton Water,* plate 10.

{118}

34 Letter from Freer to Whistler

33 Ferry Avenue.
[Detroit]
[19 July 1897]

My dear Mr. Whistler;

I am very glad to have your recent cablegram, which came during my absence from home, and am delighted to enclose herewith draft on London, for six hundred guineas, payable to your order, in partial payment for the Nocturne "Southampton."[1] I say partial payment because money cannot do more in connection with such a great work of art.

I do hope you know how deeply grateful I am to you for entrusting to my care this wonderful interpretation of the true beauty and mystery of night, also that you will pardon my inability to fully express my appreciation.

Fig. 32. Giovanni Boldini (1844–1931), *Whistler Asleep,* 1897. Drypoint (19.8 x 29.5), 06.277. "It is interesting in one way," Freer wrote to the New York dealer Frederick Keppel upon first seeing this portrait of Whistler, "but to my mind too utterly artistic to be of any value whatever" (24 December 1897, FGA Letterpress Book 4).

You are very well, I trust, and will some day come to America and give your many friends here a chance to see you, I hope.

Faithfully,
Charles L. Freer.

Detroit. July 19th 97.

GUL Whistler F447. Personal stationery.

---

1. *Nocturne in Black and Gold: Entrance to Southampton Water,* plate 10.

𝟥𝟧 Cablegram from Whistler to Freer

[Paris]

AUG. 2ND., '97

7:10 A.M.

PARIS, VIA FRENCH

FREER, DETROIT.

RECEIVED SOUTHAMPTON[1] 600 IN CHARMING LETTER.

WHISTLER.

FGA Whistler 39. Postal Telegraph-Cable Company trans-Atlantic cablegram.

---

1. *Nocturne in Black and Gold: Entrance to Southampton Water,* plate 10.

36 Letter from Whistler to Freer

> Pavillon Madeleine.
> Pourville-sur-Mer.
> pres Dieppe, France.
> [26 July 1899]

I do hope my dear Mr. Freer, that you will not go off again to America without my seeing you!—Your letter, as you see, has reached me here—

Do write me a line telling me your plans.

I am a bit of an invalide for the time—and have just been sent here by the Doctor that I may pick up again, with the sea air, and the care of the ladies of my family[1] who had taken a house for the summer.

Doubtless this will all come right again in a little while—but I was rather down with the shocking influenza—etc.—

But you? Have you been here for some time? that you speak of returning to America!

Fig. 33. *Grey and Gold: High Tide at Pourville,* 1899. Oil on panel (13.9 x 23.4), 04.163. One of several small marines Whistler painted while convalescing at Pourville-sur-Mer, France.

You cannot have been in Paris, or you would have found me of course—

Are you perhaps going again on a long journey and will perhaps be coming back on your way home?

However you will write—and I will get well as quickly as possible—

Always sincerely yours
J McNeill Whistler

FGA Whistler 42 (copy, GUL Whistler LB4:29; typescript, GUL Whistler F448). Mourning stationery. Envelope addressed to Freer at Carlton Hotel, Haymarket, London; postmarked Dieppe, 26 July 1899.

1. Whistler was attended by Beatrix Whistler's mother, Frances Philip, and her younger sister, Rosalind Birnie Philip (1873–1958), whom Whistler adopted as his ward after his wife's death in 1896 and later named executor of his estate.

37 Letter from Whistler to Freer

[Pourville-sur-Mer, France]
[29 July 1899]

I am delighted my dear Mr. Freer that you like the pictures you speak of, and wish [to] keep them.[1]

They are yours of course—and I will tell you when we meet how glad I am that they go to the group you have of distinguished work in your Gallery—

And now you must yield a point in proof of friendship and sympathy already proven!

Nothing is to be said about price in this matter—until the Blue Girl takes her place to preside[2]—

All this you will understand completely and feel with when we meet.

Meanwhile I think I may tell you without the least chance of being misunderstood, that I wish you to have a fine collection of Whistlers!! perhaps The collection—

You see the Englishmen have all sold—"for 'tis their nature to," as Dr Watts beautifully puts it[3]—whatever paintings of mine they possessed! directly they were hall marked by The French Government, and established as of value—turning over, under my very eyes, literally for thousands what they had gotten for odd pounds! So that with the few "exceptions that prove the rule," there is scarcely a canvas of mine left in the land! While you will understand the mischievous pleasure I have in "constate-ing"[4] this fact, and so placing the British Macenas[5] where he ought to be, behind the counter, & in his shop—you will also appreciate the lack of all communion between the artist and those who held his work!—and the great pleasure it gives him to look forward to other relations!—

I am glad you have the little "Cigale"—she is one of my latest pets—and of a rare type of beauty—The child herself I mean—and the painting—well the painting [ink blot] you see what I have said of it!!

The little Lady of Soho! I am glad you have chosen her too—I think before she is packed, I know of a touch I must add, and then she can follow you in the next steamer—But this I shall see when I come over—for I am getting stronger and hope perhaps next week I may be able to cross—If the pictures have left the International,[6] they will have gone to The "Company of the Butterfly" 2. Hinde Street Manchester Square.[7]

So I enclose the order.

I have written to Messr. Heinemann to send you my book! The Baronet & The Butterfly![8] You must tell me how you like my campagne, if you think it worthy of West-Point![9]

> Always sincerely,
> J McNeill Whistler

They will tell you in Hinde Street about the prints—
[enclosure]
July 29, 1899.
Please deliver to Mr. Charles L. Freer my two pictures at the International Exhibition:
    "La Cigale" &
    the little Lady Sophie of Soho.

To
Sec. "Co. of the Butterfly"
2. Hinde Street.
Manchester Square

J. McNeill Whistler
Pavillon Madeleine.
Pourville-sur-Mer.
pres Dieppe

FGA Whistler 40 (copy, GUL Whistler LB4:33–34; typescript, GUL Whistler 449). Mourning stationery. Probably sent in envelope (FGA Whistler 43) addressed to Freer at Carlton Hotel, Pall Mall, London; postmarked London, 31 July 1899. Published in Robin Spencer, ed., *Whistler: A Retrospective* (New York: Lauter Levin, 1989), 322–23; and Nigel Thorp, ed., *Whistler on Art: Selected Letters and Writings of James McNeill Whistler* (Washington, D.C.: Smithsonian Institution Press, 1994), 167–68.

———

1. *Rose and Brown: La Cigale,* plate 11, and *Rose and Gold: The Little Lady Sophie of Soho,* plate 12.

2. *Harmony in Blue and Gold: The Little Blue Girl,* plate 2.

3. Isaac Watts (1674–1748), English theologian and hymn writer, in "Against Quarreling and Fighting," *Divine Songs* (1715):
    Let dogs delight to bark and bite,
      For God hath made them so;
    Let bears and lions growl and fight,
      For 'tis their nature too.

4. From the French *constater,* to prove.

5. "Maecenas" means patron, from the Roman statesman Gaius Maecenas, a generous friend and patron of Horace and Virgil.

6. "The Second Exhibition of The International Society of Sculptors, Painters, & Gravers," Knightsbridge, London, 7 May–July 1899. The exhibition catalogue and monogram were designed by Whistler, then president of the society.

7. Whistler established the Company of the Butterfly in 1897 for the purpose of selling his works outside the studio. The venture was unsuccessful and the shop closed in 1901. See Martin Hopkinson, "Whistler's 'Company of the Butterfly,'" *Burlington Magazine* 136 (October 1994): 700–704.

8. *Eden versus Whistler: The Baronet and the Butterfly. A Valentine with a Verdict* (Paris: Louis-Henry May), published in May 1899, chronicles Whistler's quarrel with Sir William Eden over payment for a portrait of the baronet's wife, which ended in 1897 with a verdict favorable to Whistler. On 1 August 1899 a copy of the book was sent to Freer with Whistler's compliments, signed with the butterfly and inscribed: "To Charles L. Freer—a determined friend / with affection" (Rare Books Collection, FGA Library).

9. Whistler was a cadet at the U.S. Military Academy at West Point, New York, from 1851 to 1854.

𝒥𝒮 Letter from Whistler to Freer

[Pourville-sur-Mer,
France]
[4 August 1899]

Dear Mr. Freer—A line only to acknowledge your very delightful letter,[1] of which I hope next week to talk to you.

And to wonder if you have seen The Bognor at Liverpool?[2]

I am having sent to you a photogravure they have just done of the little Lady Sophie,[3] to keep her in your mind, in case she remains with me for another couple of steamers!—

I am much better again and were it not for the doctor's injunctions would run over to London directly—
However by Tuesday next—or Wednesday morning I
hope to see you—
    In great haste

                                    Very sincerely yours
                                    J McN Whistler

Have you read the book?

FGA Whistler 41 (copy, GUL Whistler LB4:35). Mourning stationery. Envelope
addressed to Freer at the Carlton Hotel, Haymarket, London; postmarked
Dieppe, 4 August 1899, and London, 5 August 1899; with notation in Freer's
hand, "ansd."

1. The letter has not survived, but Freer seems to have responded favorably
to the proposal Whistler made in letter 37.

2. Freer would purchase *Nocturne: Blue and Silver—Bognor,* plate 3, in
October from Alfred Chapman of Liverpool, who delivered it to Freer on
board his homebound steamer (Freer to N. E. Montross, 11 March 1901, FGA
Letterpress Book 7).

3. The photogravure of *Rose and Gold: The Little Lady Sophie of Soho,* plate
12, was made for the frontispiece to the Edition de Luxe of the 1899
International Society of Sculptors, Painters, & Gravers exhibition catalogue.

39 Letter from Freer to Whistler

33 Ferry Avenue.
Detroit, Michigan
June 27th, 1900.

My dear Mr. Whistler;

Your message through Mr. Marchant, of the Goupil Galleries, has just reached me and I am delighted to know that I am soon to have the beautiful portrait of the "Little Lady of Soho."[1] I have asked Mr. Marchant to attend to the packing and forwarding.[2] May I ask you to take the trouble to make the usual declaration at the U.S. Consulate, No. 12, St. Helen's Place? I dislike to put you to so much trouble, but our Custom's law requires it, or, the payment of 20% duty.

Kindly remember that I am still in your financial debt for the price of the little nude figure (a great gem) that I brought home with me last fall, the etchings sent to me by the Society of the Butterfly, and the portrait to be forwarded by Mr. Marchant.[3] Will you let me know how much I may have the pleasure of remitting? Perhaps you may have finished

Fig. 34. *Balustrade, Luxembourg Gardens* (K427), 1892–93. Etching (12.7 x 21.5), 06.123.

the two small pictures which were in your studio and which you said I might have when completed.[4] If so I would [be] glad to have them sent over with the portrait and the small water color in the possession of the Society of the Butterfly, chosen by me last summer.[5]

You are very well, I trust. What is the Paris Exhibition like?[6] Our American papers have said many pleasant things about your portrait of yourself—I would like to see it.[7]

I am thinking of visiting Capri next September, and of returning via Paris and London. Are you likely to be in either of those cities during the latter part of September or early in October?

Shall the "Little Blue Girl"[8] be ready for her trip to this side by that time?

With every good wish,

Very sincerely yours,
Charles L. Freer.

GUL Whistler F450. Personal stationery.

---

1. *Rose and Gold: The Little Lady Sophie of Soho,* plate 12.

2. Freer wrote W. S. Marchant, manager of the Goupil Gallery in London, with instructions that same day (FGA Letterpress Book 6).

3. The "little nude figure" is *Rose and Brown: La Cigale,* plate 11. The etchings are probably *Café Luxembourg* (K434), 02.119, and *Balustrade, Luxembourg Gardens* (K427), fig. 34, both shown in the "White Room" of the 1899 exhibition of the International Society of Sculptors, Painters, & Gravers. The title Freer inscribed on the back of *Balustrade, Luxembourg Gardens*—"The Terrace, Luxembourg"—matches the title of an etching exhibited in 1899; its identity is confirmed by the description Freer noted in his catalogue, "two grown people seated & children" (FGA Library), and in a memorandum of 31 August 1899, "oblong, showing group of people on a balcony" (FGA Art Invoices/Whistler/ Misc.). A registered-letter envelope addressed to Freer in Detroit and bearing numerous postmarks including London, 12 August 1899, New York, 19 August 1899, and Detroit, 21 August 1899, probably contained correspondence about the etchings from the Company of the Butterfly: it is inscribed by Freer, "Cafe Luxembourg and The Terrace Luxembourg 1899" (FGA 41A).

Freer paid Whistler for the etchings in 1902 (see letter 67).

4. Probably *Purple and Gold: Phryne the Superb!—Builder of Temples,* fig. 9, and *Writing on the Wall,* fig. 40.

5. Presumably *Chelsea Children,* plate 13. See letter 67.

6. Exposition Universelle, Paris, Fine Arts Exhibit of the United States of America, May 1900. Whistler was awarded one Grand Prix for paintings and another for etchings.

7. *Brown and Gold* (Hunterian Art Gallery, Glasgow).

8. *Harmony in Blue and Gold: The Little Blue Girl,* plate 2.

40 Telegram from Whistler to Freer

LONDON 3927 17 11
6H44
[11 October 1900]

= SHALL BE DELIGHTED TO SEE YOU AM HERE UNTIL END OCTOBER[1] = WHISTLER

FGA Whistler 44. Delivered to Freer at Hotel Windsor, Paris; stamped Paris (Bourse), 11 October 1900.

---

1. Freer would be in London from 14 to 19 October 1900.

41 Telegram from Whistler to Freer

[London]
[18 October 1900]

TO CHARLES FREER CARLTON HOTEL
SUFFERING VERY MUCH LET US POSTPONE DINNER UNTIL YOUR
RETURN WHEN YOU ALSO ARE WELL BON VOYAGE SEND LINE
WHEN ARRIVE
WHISTLER

FGA Whistler 45. Post Office telegram handed in at Tottenham Court Road
telegraph office (near Whistler's Fitzroy Street studio) at 5:57 P.M., received
6:11 P.M.; stamped Charles Street, Haymarket, SW, 18 October 1900.

42 Letter from Whistler to Freer

[London]
[19 October 1900]

Dear Mr. Freer—How very nice & kind of you in the midst
of your haste!—

Yes I am better—and the pain nearly gone!

You also I am glad to know the Doctor has taken care
of. How wise we both were!

Never mind the Carlyle—You will see him next time[1]—

And do manage <u>to stay</u> that <u>together</u> we may manage
something in the studio—

With very best wishes and again Bon voyage

Always affectionately
J McNeill Whistler

Tell me how the little Lady Sophie looks on your wall.[2]

FGA Whistler 51 (copy, GUL Whistler LB4:36). Mourning stationery. Unstamped envelope addressed to Freer at Carlton Hotel (London); with pencil notation in another hand, "1901 (?)."

---

1. Freer must have hoped to see Whistler's *Arrangement in Grey and Black, No. 2: Portrait of Thomas Carlyle* (City Art Gallery, Glasgow), then on display in Liverpool, before he sailed from that city on 20 October; see fig. 35.

2. *Rose and Gold: The Little Lady Sophie of Soho,* plate 12. After arranging in June to send the painting to Freer (see letter 39), Whistler had asked (through W. S. Marchant) to keep it for a future exhibition; Freer replied that as he had already waited a year for the picture, he would prefer to have it with him during the winter in Detroit (Freer to Marchant, 11 August 1900, FGA Letterpress Book 6). Apparently, Freer took the painting home in 1900, with the understanding that he would lend it to Whistler for exhibition in Paris the following year (see letter 44).

Fig. 35. Henry Wolf (1852–1916), after Whistler's *Arrangement in Grey and Black, No. 2: Portrait of Thomas Carlyle* (City Art Gallery, Glasgow). Wood engraving (22.6 x 19.1), 04.430.

43 Letter from Freer to Whistler

33 Ferry Avenue.
Detroit, Michigan.
Decem. 1st, 1900

Dear Mr. Whistler,

Since my return home I have found it necessary to spend much of my time in New York and Boston and less than one week ago was the first opportunity I had to unpack and hang in your group the "Little Lady Sophie of Soho."[1]

I found that the journey had fortunately done her no harm and that she was as attractive as ever. Along with "The Balcony," "Bognor," "Portsmouth Harbour" (Nocturne), "La Cigale"[2] and the delightful water colors and pastels, she hangs in serene triumph, a bit coquettish perhaps, but always beautiful. She has many admirers already and the number is sure to increase.

I am positive that I have never thanked you sufficiently for having placed her in my care and I fear that I never can.

Your health is very much improved I hope. Do take the best of care of yourself and accept I beg you, my renewed appreciation of your many courtesies extended during my recent visit in London. I am quite well again and am anticipating a very pleasant winter.

With every good wish and kindest regards,
Believe me,

Faithfully yours,
Charles L. Freer

GUL Whistler F451. Personal stationery.

---

1. *Rose and Gold: The Little Lady Sophie of Soho,* plate 12.

2. The four paintings Freer refers to are *Variations in Flesh Colour and Green: The Balcony,* plate 1, *Nocturne: Blue and Silver—Bognor,* plate 3, *Nocturne in Black and Gold: Entrance to Southampton Water,* plate 10 (which Freer calls "Portsmouth Harbour"), and *Rose and Brown: La Cigale,* plate 11.

44 Letter from Whistler to Freer

Ajaccio.
Feb. 10. 1901.

Dear Mr. Freer—You will be amused to find me calmly writing from Bounaparte's Island![1]

Happily you know that it is not my way to seek my effects in the glories of others!—Still "Napoleon and I". . . . Enfin!—

Curiously enough you speak of this health of mine—and it is in its supposed interest that I am away from my work shops, and have wandered so far seeking sun & warmth!

We were neither of us very well when last together in town—and I am glad to know that your voyage has restored you completely—For myself the doctor refused all medicine—"You want no drugs," he said, "a trip at sea—and the rest that you never take is your affair!"—and for two months I have been attempting this rest—Upon my word I don't think I manage it well—and I wish I had gone with you to Detroit! I shall know better another time!

I am delighted to hear that the little Lady Sophie has been behaving so well in her new country![2]

And now it is time to think about the exhibition in Paris we talked over together[3]—I should like then the pastels and the water colour figures, The Bognor, & the Lady Sophie, & La Cigale, the "Southampton" Harbour (not Portsmouth) has already been exhibited in Europe.[4]

Now I want much to make a beautiful show of the etchings—& if you can send me a chosen set of your proofs of course it will be perfect. The lithographs I think I have, or can borrow in England—

I shall write Mrs. Gardner for some of her pictures—& pastels[5]—and also to Mansfield—

Among your dry points, you have a fine proof, have you not? of Annie Haden?—I mean the large full length in the cloak and hat?[6]

I need not tell you that I shall be deeply grateful to you for this you know—but it seems to express so miserably my sense of this most charming act of friendship and courtesy & kindness on your part!

Fig. 36. *Annie Haden* (K62), 1860. Drypoint, third state (34.8 x 21.4), 98.297. Inscribed by Freer, verso, "Finished state." This was among the works Freer purchased in 1898, a collection formerly in the possession of Annie's father (and Whistler's brother-in-law), Francis Seymour Haden.

I shall write again directly—but this little note I send off at once—for this place seems so oddly away from all usual routes, that I, who am, in the midst of this ridiculous idleness, filled with a new nervousness, fancy that not a day should be lost!—

Write to me always addressing Rue du Bac—and if I had a telegram to send I suppose that Freer, Detroit would reach you all right of course.

This Mediterranean business of Summer sky & Southern atmosphere is, entre nous, all nonsense!—

And as I said the other day shows how little people know about climate at all! In short I have been simply frozen! and indeed, once for all, there is nothing Southern but the South! and I ought to have gone to the West Indies immediately!

This place is full of beautiful things for panels or plates—but directly I look at one of them and stand for a moment, some mistral or tra montana[7] blows me into the hotel with a new little cold that just prevents my getting back to Paris!

These winter "resorts" might be quite tolerable in the Summer!

Always, believe me,

affectionately yrs
J McNeill Whistler

FGA Whistler 46 (copy, GUL Whistler LB4:27–28; typescript, GUL Whistler F452). Mourning stationery. Probably sent in envelope (FGA 43) addressed to Freer at 33 Ferry Avenue, Detroit; postmarked Ajaccio and Marseilles, 11 February 1901.

1. From January until mid-February 1901, Whistler was convalescing in Ajaccio, the French city on the Mediterranean island of Corsica, where Napoléon Bonaparte was born.

2. *Rose and Gold: The Little Lady Sophie of Soho,* plate 12.

3. Whistler seems to have planned to send some of the works to the Palais des Beaux-Arts on the Champ de Mars, the venue for exhibitions of the Société Nationale des Beaux-Arts, and then to a solo exhibition he planned to hold at the Goupil Gallery in Paris. See letter 47.

4. The paintings Whistler refers to are *Nocturne: Blue and Silver—Bognor,* plate 3, *Rose and Gold: The Little Lady Sophie of Soho,* plate 12, *Rose and Brown: La Cigale,* plate 11, and *Nocturne in Black and Gold: Entrance to Southampton Water,* plate 10. *Nocturne in Black and Gold* had been shown in London at the Grosvenor Gallery in 1882 and possibly at the Goupil Gallery in 1892.

5. Isabella Stewart Gardner (1840–1924) assembled an outstanding, eclectic art collection and built an Italianate gallery in Boston to house it. She owned three Whistler oil paintings and several pastels, including a pastel portrait of herself.

6. *Annie Haden* (K62), fig. 36.

7. *Tramontana* is Italian for a fierce north wind.

45 Letter from Freer to Whistler

33 Ferry Avenue.
Detroit.
March 6th 1901

Dear Mr. Whistler;

I am sorry to learn from your letter written at Ajaccio that the dreadful cold from which you was suffering when I saw you last in London has clung to you all of these months and is still annoying you.

How very unfortunate! And with it all to think of wasting so many ice girt days in a land supposed to blossom with passion-flowers and languish with sunshine. Surely it is all too cruel and faithless!

Yes, and I quite agree with your opinion of the average winter resorts; to me they are like huge pickled monsters, half asleep, but always ready to breathe out frosted air, whisper in hurricanes and whirl black water in ones pathway.

But your health is much improved 'ere this, I hope, and you are safely back again in Paris, I trust.

Do take the best of care of yourself and when next in search of a sunny restful land try the real south and journey thither via Detroit.

Now, concerning your proposed exhibition to be held in Paris next spring, of course, I will be most happy to send of your work in my possession—and you remember it was agreed between us in London, last October, that the little "Lady Sophie" was to visit Paris in the spring—And she, little Lady that she is, will be glad to face the fair Parisiennes on their own ground. "La Cigale" too, will smile benignly upon all. "Bognor," I regret to say is promised for an exhibition to open in New York next week and from there it is to go to Buffalo for the Pan-American Exhibition lasting till October next, so I cannot include it with the Paris lot.[1]

I can however, let you have the following pastels:[2]—

"Harmony in Blue and Violet" 1890–1
   (Tite Street Studio)
"A Violet Note" 1895
   (Paris)
"Rose and Red. The little Red Cap" "
   (Paris)
   Water Color
"Blue and Gold. The Rose Azalea" "
   (Paris)

As to etchings, how would the list enclosed herein suit?

I can add to it or take from it just as you would care to have me do—or, if you prefer I can, I think fill almost any list you may send excepting a few of the early and excessively rare dry points.

And now a word or two concerning shipping—Shall they be addressed to Rue du Bac or have you an Agent in Paris to receive them?

And how soon must they start?

Where and when will the exhibition be held? I should like very much to see it and if possible I will arrange to do so on my way to or from Capri, and I hope at the same time I may have the pleasure of seeing you again and that I will then find you perfectly well and happy.

Here in Detroit we are enjoying a real old fashioned winter with splendid sleighing, and beautiful dry clear cold days.

As ever,

Most affectionately,
Charles L. Freer

P.S. My cable address is
Freer
Detroit—

[enclosure]

w. 47³ Arthur Seymour [*Arthur Haden* (κ61)],
w. 48   Becquet [κ52],
w. 53   Drouet [κ55],
w. 57   Annie Haden [κ62, fig. 36]
w. 83   Weary [κ92],
w. 144 The "Adam and Eve": Old Chelsea [κ175],
w. 149 Little Venice [κ183],
w. 168 Nocturne Palaces [κ202],
w. 189 The Dyer [κ219],
w. 242 Dipping the Flag [κ325],
w. 247 Windsor—Dry Point
        [*Windsor (Memorial)* (κ329)],
w. 259 Mairie, Loches [κ382],
w. 260 Steps, Amsterdam [κ403, fig. 1],
w. 262 The Balcony, Amsterdam [κ405],
w. 265 Nocturne—Dance House [κ408, fig. 16],
w. 266 Long House, Dyer's Amsterdam [κ406],
        The Mill [κ413],
        The Lace Curtain [κ410, plate 7],
        Hotel de Ville, Loches [κ384],
        Chateau Amboise [κ393],
        Tower of St. Antoine [κ392],
        Clock Tower of S. Amboise [κ394],
        Courtyard Rue De La Courier [κ368],
        Blois Cathedral [κ397],
        Chancellerie [κ383],
        From the Walk of Agnes Sorel [κ385],
        Hotel Allemand
        [*Hôtel Lallement, Bourges* (κ399), fig. 37],
        Station Voves [κ371],
        Doorway, Chapel of Montresor [κ395],
        Cameo No. 1 [κ347, fig. 20].

GUL Whistler F454 (typescript copy, "Memorandum from letter to Mr. Whistler, dated March 6, 1901," FGA Letterpress Book 7). Personal stationery. Typescript copy of enclosure with notation in Freer's hand, "List of Whistler Etchings enclosed in letter to him of March 6th," FGA Letterpress Book 7.

---

1. *Rose and Gold: The Little Lady Sophie of Soho,* plate 12, *Rose and Brown: La Cigale,* plate 11, and *Nocturne: Blue and Silver—Bognor,* plate 3. The Nocturne was included in a small exhibition of twelve paintings at the Montross Gallery, 372 Fifth Avenue, New York, before its exhibition in Buffalo, New York, at the Pan-American Exposition, Division of Fine Arts, 1 May to 1 November 1901.

2. The four works Freer refers to are *Harmony in Blue and Violet,* plate 6, *A Violet Note—Spring,* plate 4, *Rose and Red: The Little Pink Cap,* plate 9, and *Blue and Gold—The Rose Azalea,* plate 8.

3. Freer identifies the prints by their numbers in Frederick Wedmore's *Whistler's Etchings: A Study and a Catalogue,* 2d ed. (London: Colnaghi, 1889), which would be superseded in 1910 by Edward G. Kennedy's comprehensive catalogue of Whistler's etchings.

Fig. 37. *Hôtel Lallement, Bourges* (K399), 1888. Etching (16.4 x 26.8), 03.212. Inscribed by Whistler, verso, "1st state. Early proof," and signed with the butterfly. Freer purchased this print from Wunderlich & Co., New York, in 1889.

Detroit, Michigan,
March 28th, 1901.

Memorandum for Mr. Whistler.

Under the Custom Laws of the United States, objects of art sent to foreign countries for exhibition and return must be accompanied on their homeward journey by consular invoices showing the name and price of each article.

The list attached hereto covers the paintings and prints shipped to Messrs. Goupil & Company of Paris. The titles are complete, covering two paintings in oil, one painting in water color, three pastels, and thirty etchings. The prices paid by Mr. Freer are shown complete, with two exceptions, namely: the two paintings in oil.[1] For these Mr. Freer is still indebted to Mr. Whistler. Will Mr. Whistler kindly enter approximate values for these two art works opposite their respective titles. Will Mr. Whistler also kindly visit the American Consular Office in Paris, and make usual statement concerning the authenticity of these objects of art at the time they are returned to America.

Typescript copy, FGA Letterpress Book 7.

———————

1. The works by Whistler to which Freer refers are listed in letter 45.

[Ajaccio]
[late April 1901]

Dear Mr. Freer—I have just received notice from Goupils Paris, of the safe arrival of the Etchings Pastels & Etchings —Again how kind of you!

The pictures are, it is true, too late for the Champs de Mars, where I had hoped to send them[1]—Still they have never been seen in France, and will be beautifully & becomingly shown—when the exhibition is properly organised.

You see I did not take into my calculations this question of health!—and you perceive that I still write from this Island so difficult to leave!

However definitely I ~~return~~ take the boat for Marseilles on Wednesday,[2] and return to Paris via London! on the P & O Steamer, so that I may complete the benefit of the long absence by another sea trip and appear in great condition in my work shops again.

And now what do you think ~~has been at all the trouble with me~~

The truth that I have discovered here & that has so filled me with delight—weighed with a certain resentment which you

Fig. 38. *Bohemians, Corsica* (K442), 1901. Etching (8.4 x 5.3), 03.94. Inscribed by Freer, verso, "Hole in the wall—Ajaccio." One of the last four etchings of Whistler's career, this is the only Corsica print in the Freer collection. Freer bought it from Robert Dunthorne of London in 1903.

will presently understand—is that <u>nothing</u> is ~~physically~~ the matter with me & my physical health! No wonder the London doctor who is a good fellow, for an Englishman, said "you want no medicine, go away, & rest and amuse yourself and come back fit for everything!"

Yes but he stopped short of the real matter & his prescribed "rest" & amusement—He did not know what I myself was not conscious of, that I have never "amused" myself! that for <u>years</u> I have <u>never</u> rested! Never as one should say sat down! never taken a "holiday"! never permitted myself a Saturday afternoon! For <u>years</u>. Think of it!

All work & no play made of Jack a dull boy! and dull indeed have I been—for I have never played!

and I ~~never had~~ not even a sense of the meaning of "rest"—nor did I at all know of the real [illegible] to myself such ignorance inevitably entailed!

And in this wild pursuit of work the machine ~~was terribly strained~~ This beautiful & sensitive machine, "not much [illegible]" was [illegible] overworked and strained—

GUL Whistler F453. The letter apparently was neither completed nor sent.

1. The Champ de Mars was the site of the Palais des Beaux-Arts, venue for exhibitions of the Société Nationale des Beaux-Arts in Paris.

2. Whistler left Corsica on 1 May 1901.

48 Letter from Freer to Whistler

Villa Castello,
Capri, Italy.
June 20th, 1901.

From the above address you will see my dear Mr. Whistler, that I too am in close communion with the mediterranean; but fortunately, drawn hither in search of beauty and idleness—not health. And then, I have a warm old time friend here, and a few pleasant acquaintances.[1]

There is no chill in the refreshing north winds and the sun is not too warm for plenty of exercise. The flowers and verdure of this interesting island are as wonderful as ever, and I often think of you and wish that your experience of last winter on Corsica might have been as delightful as mine here during the past three weeks.

Did the cold days mentioned in your last letter continue? Did you remain at Ajaccio long? And did your health improve? I earnestly hope you get rid of that miserable cold and that you are entirely well now.

Shall you be in Paris the last week of July, hardly I fear, as probably the summer heat will at that time be at its very worst?

Has your exhibition been held? I have watched the newspapers for word

Fig. 39. Freer at the Villa Castello in Capri, 1901.

concerning it but have learned nothing therefrom.

I intend to remain here until July 1st and then go to Germany for about three weeks after which spend one week in Paris and sail for America from Cherbourg on July 31st—

It would give me much pleasure indeed to see you again, even if for an hour only, and if you ~~will~~ are to be in Paris during the time before mentioned, and will let me know, I will be happy to call upon you. My address will be as at the head of this note until June 30th. Thereafter, c/o Brown, Shipley & Co. London, who will forward my mail.

With every good wish, I remain,

always faithfully yours,
Charles L. Freer.

J. A. McN. Whistler, Esq.
London.

GUL Whistler F455.

---

1. Freer had recently purchased the villa with his Detroit friend Thomas Spencer Jerome (1864–1914), consular agent in Capri from 1901. Among his other friends in Capri was the American artist Charles Caryl Coleman (1840–1928).

49   Letter from Whistler to Freer

Garlant's Hotel,
Suffolk Street, Pall Mall.[1]
[London]
[10 July 1901]

My dear Freer—I am looking forward with such pleasure to seeing you!

And there are endless things to impart—And letters are so impossible—excepting always that I was delighted to get your own.

I felt though that you were again slipping through my fingers—and escaping to America without the two or three weeks' quiet in which to go together over what I fancy interesting in both studios since last we met—Besides I have my plan! and hurry is an abomination.

Now you, who are making for yourself beautiful places and filling them with things rare and chosen, must know this better than the racing ones of Chicago! of whose mad existence I have been reading—And you will put off your return—changing from one steamer to another at your own pleasant will—until we two shall have talked together at our ease, &, to our exceeding satisfaction, as becomes those of our distinction, for whom breathless words of greeting & parting should scarcely be mingled over the same shaking of hands!—

The little Lady Sophie is holding her Court in all honour in Munich for the moment[2]—and the pastels & proofs are all safe with me, waiting for the exhibition. Brown Shipley have not as yet had your address or I would have wired before now—

They tell me though that they expect you here any day—Excellent!

Let me hear from you directly you get this—

Always sincerely

FGA 47 (copy, GUL Whistler LB4:30). Hotel letterhead. Envelope addressed to Freer care of Messrs. Brown Shipley & Co., Pall Mall (London), and forwarded to Grand Hotel Continental, Munich; postmarked London, 10 July 1901, and Munich, 12 July 1901; with notation in Freer's hand, "answd July 21st Dresden."

---

1. Whistler stayed at Garlant's Hotel after his return from Corsica.

2. *Rose and Gold: The Little Lady Sophie of Soho,* plate 12, was shown at the VIII *Internationale Kunst-Austellung* (8th International Art Exposition), Königlichen Glaspalast, 1 June–31 October 1901.

50 Letter from Freer to Whistler

Weber's Hôtel,
Dresden.
July 21st, 1901

Dear Mr. Whistler;

Your good letter reached me a few days ago at Munich and I was delighted to hear from you.

I would have answered at once but I could not determine my plans until the arrival of friends with whom I was to visit and until I received word from America concerning my sisters health; she having recently suffered from a stroke of paralysis. I am most happy to say that she seems sure of recovery but I feel it my duty to hurry home.[1] Therefore, I cannot accept your kind suggestion to put off my return to America "changing from steamer to steamer" as I would, under other conditions, enjoy doing.[2]

I must be in Berlin to morrow and next day, and it may be necessary for me to go to Hamburg immediately thereafter, so I am unlikely to reach Paris before the 27th inst.

On the 31st inst. my steamer the Kaiserin Maria Theresia sails from Cherbourg and I feel that because of my sisters health I really must abandon all thought of prolonging my stay on this side of the Atlantic.

You are so good to say that I might go with you over the work in your two studios, and nothing I am sure, would give me more delight—but I cannot, I regret, reach London this year. Shall you be in Paris between the 27th and 30th inst.? I fear not, especially because of the extreme heat of which I have heard so much.

And then as you wrote, the "breathless words of greet- ing and parting" rushed through so short a space of time are always unsatisfying. Still, it's better than nothing, and if you should be in Paris at the time mentioned I would be happy to see you.

I have most charming memories of my visits to your studios and the works you have so kindly allowed me to carry away are my chief trea- sures. I can never sufficiently thank you.

I was most happily sur- prised in walking through the exhibition at Munich, before the receipt of your letter, to find enthroned upon a special pedestal, in a perfect light, the

Fig. 40. *Writing on the Wall,* ca. 1894–1902. Pastel on brown paper (27.5 x 18.0), 02.113. Although this pastel was probably begun at the same time as *A Violet Note—Spring,* plate 4, which it resembles, Whistler still had not finished it to his satisfaction in 1902, when Freer bought it.

Little Lady Sophie,[3] who by her rare charm was the saving grace of a conventional exhibition. Your lithographs too, saved another room—but the affair as a whole is deadly! Acres of meaningless canvas—and crowds of brainless observers![4]

That wonderful drawing of the lady writing upon the wall, and the other works in progress, seen in your London studio last year still linger most delightfully in my mind.[5] And the "Little Blue Girl"[6] how is she? and when may I take her to reign in her future home?

With best wishes,

Always sincerely,
Charles L. Freer

P.S. My Paris address is care Windsor Hotel, Rue de Rivoli.

GUL Whistler F456. Hotel letterhead.

---

1. Emma Frances ("Frank") Freer (1845–1915), Freer's eldest sibling and only sister, lived all her life in Kingston, New York. The previous day Freer had heard from Hecker of her "continued improvement" (see Freer to Hecker, from Dresden, 21 July 1901, FGA Hecker).

2. Freer wrote to Hecker from Munich, "Friends from America now on this side have kindly urged me to change steamers and return with them. Whistler wants me to give him three weeks in Paris and London, 'I have plans' he writes, but to them all I have said nay, for indeed I am far from starved, my cup is already full, and home and enjoyment there of what the Gods have so abundantly strewn in my path will I am sure surpass all else" (15 July 1901, FGA Hecker).

3. *Rose and Gold: The Little Lady Sophie of Soho,* plate 12.

4. Freer wrote to Hecker, "To my surprise I find the present exhibition of modern international art very instructive; beautiful in no sense, and saved by complete rottenness by Whistler, [John Singer] Sargent, [Gari] Melchers, and a few others, but valuable in showing to what depths of imbecility the great horde of modern painters have fallen. 'The Little Lady Soho' presides in honor in the principal court upon a throne of her own" (15 July 1901, FGA Hecker).

5. Freer refers to *Writing on the Wall,* fig. 40, and presumably to *Purple and Gold: Phryne the Superb!—Builder of Temples,* fig. 9. See letter 39.

6. *Harmony in Blue and Gold: The Little Blue Girl,* plate 2.

51 Whistler's calling card, inscribed to Freer

[London]
[23 July 1901]

greatly intrigued & disappointed at receiving no reply to letter—

Most anxious to see you.

Garlant's Hotel.
Tuesday 23. July

FGA Whistler 43-a. Card (mourning), imprinted, "Mr. J. McNeill Whistler, / Cheyne Walk, Chelsea. / 110, Rue du Bac." Inscription recto and verso.

52 Telegram from Whistler to Freer

P LONDON 2829 17
27/7 8-27-
[27 July 1901]

= PROPOSE DINING WITH YOU TOMORROW PLEASE ORDER ROOM YOUR HOTEL = WHISTLER +

FGA Whistler 48. Delivered to Freer at Hotel Windsor, rue de Rivoli, Paris; stamped Paris (Bourse), 27 July 1901.

53 Telegram from Whistler to Freer

PARIS CALAIS 8982 13
28 3/29 S
[28 July 1901]

+ TRAIN DELAYED HOPE VVONT SPOIL DINNER[1] + VVHISTTER

FGA Whistler 49. Delivered to Freer at Hotel Windsor, rue de Rivoli, Paris; stamped Paris (Central and Av. de l'Opera), 28 July 1901; with inscription, "Calais."

---

1. According to Freer's pocket diary, Whistler arrived in Paris at 8 o'clock that evening.

54 Letter from Rosalind Philip to Freer

8. Fitzroy Street. W.
[London]
Oct. 25th 1901.

Dear Mr. Freer.

Mr. Whistler who is at his easel wishes me to write a line to catch to-day's steamer. He is talking and I am writing.

"I think I had better enclose the letter just received from Mr. Cowan.[1] You see then that he is going to sell his Whistlers and as they are what you really ought to have I am writing to him to try & hold in until he shall have heard from you. I certainly advise you to secure these things, or in any case two of them, that is "The Thames in Ice" and the water colour picture of "Mrs. Whibley."[2]

They will cost money but I should be sorry to know they went anywhere else.

Besides I think you will never forgive yourself if you miss them.

In your collection moreover everything that you add, of this quality, goes to increase the value of what is already there, and I know that you ought certainly not to miss these two.

Mr. Cowan was asking £2.000 some time ago for "The Thames in Ice," but managed to hang on to it. However I suppose things are pretty bad just now over here and you may as well get the pictures without paying Marchant or Thomson[3] their commission.

Fig. 41. *Needlework* (w113), 1896. Lithograph (19.4 x 14.3), 02.124. A portrait of Rosalind Birnie Philip that Freer purchased from the Company of the Butterfly in 1900.

If I were you then I would cable to him, and ask him if he can hold on long enough to send you photographs, unless you take my advice, and buy them "in a poke."[4] Remember it was in this way Kennedy got "The Balcony" for you.[5] As I have never heard any more about the Paris Bernheim pictures, that the Courier was so sure of, I suppose nothing came of it."[6]

"This must go now so good bye for the present."

With kindest regards
from me also.
R. Birnie-Philip.

FGA Whistler 50 (copy, GUL Whistler LB4:37–38; typescript, GUL Whistler P459). Mourning stationery.

---

1. John James Cowan (1846–1936) was an Edinburgh industrialist and art collector. He had written on 24 October 1901 to inform Whistler that he was preparing to sell a few works from his collection. (A typescript copy of the letter with a note that the original was returned to Whistler on 11 November 1901 is in FGA Cowan.)

2. *The Thames in Ice,* plate 14, and *Rose and Silver: Portrait of Mrs. Whibley,* plate 15. Ethel Philip Whibley (1861–1920), sister of Beatrix Whistler and Rosalind Philip, posed for a number of portraits before her marriage in 1894 to the American writer Charles Whibley (1860–1930).

3. David Croal Thomson (1855–1930) of the Goupil Gallery, London, had masterminded Whistler's 1892 exhibition.

4. At Whistler's urging, Cowan wrote Freer on 1 November 1901 advising him of the price of the pictures—£2,000 (approximately $10,000) for *The Thames in Ice* and £400 ($2,000) for *Portrait of Mrs. Whibley*—and assuring him that they had not been offered to anyone else (FGA Cowan). Freer, who was in New York, did not receive the letter until 10 November; by then he had cabled Cowan for the price of the pictures and accepted his offer (11 November 1901, FGA Letterpress Book 8).

5. *Variations in Flesh Colour and Green: The Balcony,* plate 1. On Whistler's advice, Edward G. Kennedy had purchased *The Balcony* (together with three other paintings) from John Cavafy in June 1892 for £650, on the condition that Kennedy return *Harmony in Blue and Silver: Trouville* (Isabella Stewart Gardner Museum, Boston) to Whistler (Whistler to Kennedy, 10 June 1892, Edward Guthrie Kennedy Papers, New York Public Library).

6. In his letter to Whistler, Cowan alluded to a group of unfinished paintings Whistler seems to have sold to the Paris art dealer Charles Hessele, who sold them in turn to another dealer, George Bernheim. Recognizing how incomplete they were, Whistler subsequently attempted to retrieve the pictures, referring to them as "defective and purloined"; when Bernheim threatened to sue Whistler for slander, the matter was dropped (Andrew McLaren Young, Margaret MacDonald, Robin Spencer, and Hamish Miles, *The Paintings of James McNeill Whistler* [New Haven: Yale University Press, 1980], cat. no. 437).

55 Cablegram from Freer to Whistler

[New York City]
Nov 8 [1901]

WHISTLER
8 FITZROY STREET LONDON

HAVE PURCHASED THE TWO PICTURES[1] FROM COWAN MANY
THANKS WRITING
FREER

FGA Cowan 10. MS copy.

———————

1. *The Thames in Ice,* plate 14, and *Rose and Silver: Portrait of Mrs. Whibley,*
plate 15.

56 Letter from Freer to Rosalind Philip

33 Ferry Avenue.
Detroit, Michigan.
November 9th, 1901.

Dear Miss Philip,

It was very kind indeed to write me so fully at Mr.
Whistler's request, and I want to thank you most heartily for
your goodness.

You will be glad to know that two of the Cowan pictures
are to be guarded in the future by me.[1]

I wish that some time you would come with Mr.
Whistler and see them in their new resting place. They will
never again be "on the market."

With kindest regards—
Charles L. Freer

GUL Whistler 457. Personal stationery. Envelope addressed to Philip care of Whistler, 8 Fitzroy Street, London, and forwarded to 36 Tite Street, Chelsea (where Rosalind lived with her mother in 1901); postmarked Detroit, 11 November 1901, New York, 12 November 1901, and London, 21 November 1901.

---

1. *The Thames in Ice,* plate 14, and *Rose and Silver: Portrait of Mrs. Whibley,* plate 15.

57 Letter from Freer to Whistler

33 Ferry Avenue
Detroit, Michigan
February 6th, 1902.

Dear Mr. Whistler:—

Ever since the arrival of "The Thames in Ice" and the "Portrait of Mrs. Whibley" I have been wanting to write to you and tell you how delighted I am to be priveleged to add two such important examples of your work to my little group[1]—

I shall make no attempt to tell you how delightfully I am impressed by them, but I do want you to know that I appreciate most highly your goodness in putting me in communication with Mr. Cowan and thus enabling me to obtain the pictures. I also desire to thank you most heartily for your kindness in connection with the consular invoices.

From a note recently received from Mr. Marchant I am sorry to learn that you are not enjoying good health— I trust that the disturbance was of a fleeting nature, that it has left you ere this, and that you are entirely well by this time.

Do take the very best care of yourself.

With every good wish,

Faithfully yours,
Charles L. Freer

GUL Whistler F458. Personal stationery.

---

1. *The Thames in Ice,* plate 14, and *Rose and Silver: Portrait of Mrs. Whibley,* plate 15.

58 Letter from Freer to Whistler

33 Ferry Avenue
Detroit, Michigan,
February 20th, 1902

Dear Mr. Whistler:

Ever since the time I first saw your nocturne owned by Mr. Rawlinson, I have hungered to add it to my little group of your work. Under the advice of Mr. Marchant I once offered £1.500 for the painting, which was refused.[1]

I was recently informed that an offer of £2.000 would probably be accepted. I have today written Mr. Marchant authorizing him to, if possible buy it for me at this price i.e. £2.000 net, to Mr. R. and in addition a commission of 10% to Mr. Marchant.[2]

I hope to secure it. Now, if fortune favors this effort, I am wondering if I may again impose upon your valuable time and kind patience in the matter of those dreadful consular invoices—What an annoying and unnecessary bother it is!

Uncle Sam's treasury is already overflowing to an extent beyond the powers of the politicians to absorb, and still the duty upon works of art clings like a viper.

How are you standing the winter days? Sturdily I hope, and with increasing interest in all things beautiful, I trust.

Coppers, bank failures and other similar ills have jarred financial matters over here, but not enough to prevent the enjoyment a great many people have realized in studying your great picture brought out by Kennedy. As yet, I have not been priveleged to see it but hope to 'ere long.[3]

"The Thames in Ice" and the little portrait of Mrs. Whibley have, however, helped to console me[4]—

I am hoping to be in London early in May. Shall you be in town then?

With every good wish to yourself and Miss Philip, I am

> Very sincerely
> Charles L. Freer

GUL Whistler F459. Personal stationery.

---

1. Freer and W. S. Marchant had gone together to see *Nocturne: Blue and Silver—Battersea Reach,* plate 16, at the Holland Park residence of William George Rawlinson (b. 1840), a noted print collector and an old friend of Mansfield's (Freer to Marchant, 20 February 1902, FGA Letterpress Book 9). On 12 October 1899 Freer wrote to Marchant that he was interested in acquiring it (FGA Letterpress Book 5). Freer considered the price of £2,000 too high, but he thought he might pay it since he needed the picture to "help balance" his group (19 December 1899). He made the offer of £1,500 on 1 January 1900 (Freer to Marchant, FGA Letterpress Book 8).

2. On 20 February 1902, Freer informed Marchant that his "hunger for the Whistler Nocturne owned by Mr. Rawlinson" had not diminished, and that despite the price he had decided to buy the "extraordinarily fine example of Mr. Whistler's nocturne work" (FGA Letterpress Book 9). Rawlinson was at first reluctant to part with the picture, but Marchant persuaded him to accept Freer's offer on 8 April (Marchant to Freer, 11 April 1902, FGA Marchant; and Freer to Marchant, 8 April 1902, FGA Letterpress Book 9).

3. *Mother of Pearl and Silver: The Andalusian* (National Gallery of Art, Washington, D.C.), a portrait of Ethel Whibley. Freer wrote his friend and business associate William K. Bixby (1872–1934) of St. Louis that the picture had been brought to New York by a dealer and "sold at the drop of the hat to a nephew of [Alfred Atmore] Pope of Cleveland, a Mr. [J. Harris] Whittemore, for fifteen thousand dollars. I knew nothing about the picture being in this country until it had been sold, but am very familiar with it, having seen it in Mr. Whistler's studio during its progress, and two years ago, after it was finished, I saw it in a Paris exhibition," the Exposition Universelle in 1900 (7 February 1902, FGA Letterpress Book 9).

4. *The Thames in Ice,* plate 14, and *Rose and Silver: Portrait of Mrs. Whibley,* plate 15.

59 Draft of a letter from Whistler to Freer

[Probably February or
March 1902]

Dear Mr. Freer—I shall be so glad to see you—and this time I hope there will be some <u>rest</u> about your visit!—That we may be more together—

There is much to show you and to say—

It pleases me immensely that you should have the Rawlinson Nocturne[1]—Another canvas out of England!— and with its fellows, in your sympathetic care—and I am so delighted to know that [MS breaks off]

GUL Whistler F460. Mourning stationery. The letter apparently was neither completed nor sent.

———————————

1. *Nocturne: Blue and Silver—Battersea Reach,* plate 16, formerly owned by W. G. Rawlinson.

60 Telegram from Whistler to Freer

[London]
[6 May 1902]

CHARLES FRERE

CARLTON HOTEL HAYMKT

DO DRIVE HERE NOW SO PLEASED SEE YOU NEW CHELSEA

STUDIO 74 CHEYNE WALK

WHISTLER[1]

FGA Whistler 52. Post Office telegram handed in at Chelsea telegraph office at 4:25 P.M., received 4:30 P.M.; stamped Charles Street, Haymarket, SW, 6 May 1902.

---

1. In April 1902, Whistler leased 74 Cheyne Walk, a house designed by C. R. Ashbee (1863–1942); he would live there with Rosalind Philip and her mother until his death. Freer wrote to Hecker on 6 May 1902 that he had just spent an hour with Whistler, who was insisting on painting his portrait: "I have declined, but he says he must have his way this time. I wonder if I shall be foolish enough to let him waste valuable time upon a valueless theme! I hope not" (FGA Hecker).

61 Telegram from Whistler to Freer

[London]
[13 May 1902]

FREER CARLTON HOTEL

HAYMKET

LOOK IN ABOUT THREE BRING BROWN JACKET[1]

WHISTLER

FGA Whistler 53. Post Office telegram handed in at Tottenham Court Road telegraph office (near Whistler's Fitzroy Street studio) at 12:16(?) P.M., received 12:27 P.M.; stamped Charles Street, Haymarket, SW, 13 May 1902.

———————

1. Presumably to wear when sitting for *Portrait of Charles Lang Freer,* plate 5.

62 Telegram from Whistler to Freer

[London]
[15 May 1902]

FREER CARLTON HOTEL HAYMKT
NOT WELL ENOUGH TO VENTURE OUT TO-DAY PERHAPS YOU
WILL LOOK IN
WHISTLER

FGA Whistler 54. Post Office telegram handed in at King's Road telegraph office (near Whistler's home in Chelsea) at 1:35 P.M., received 1:57 P.M.; stamped Charles Street, Haymarket, SW, 15 May 1902.

63 Telegram from Whistler to Freer

[London]
[16 May 1902]

FREER CARLTON HOTEL
HAYMKT
DO LOOK IN ABOUT THREE WITH JACKET[1] CHELSEA STUDIO
WHISTLER

FGA Whistler 55. Post Office telegram handed in at King's Road telegraph office at 11:28 A.M., received 11:46 A.M.; stamped Charles Street, Haymarket, SW, 16 May 1902.

---

1. Freer later wrote to John James Cowan that Whistler had not gone very far with his portrait (plate 5), but that it was, "even in its incomplete state, a wonderful example" (13 October 1902, FGA Letterpress Book 9).

64 Telegram from Whistler to Freer

[London]
[2 June 1902]

FREER CARLTON HOTEL

HAYMKT

VANDERBILT[1] SITTING THIS AFTERNOON SHALL I DINE WITH YOU TONIGHT[2]

WHISTLER

FGA Whistler 57. Post Office telegram handed in at King's Road telegraph office at 2:15 P.M., received 2:38 P.M.; stamped Charles Street, Haymarket, SW, 2 June 1902.

---

1. George Washington Vanderbilt (1862–1914), grandson of the railroad baron Cornelius Vanderbilt, collector of art—primarily Rembrandt etchings—and owner of Biltmore, an enormous estate in North Carolina. Whistler's *Portrait of George W. Vanderbilt* (National Gallery of Art, Washington, D.C.) was commissioned in 1897 but remained unfinished upon the artist's death.

2. Whistler and Freer were celebrating the end of the Anglo-Boer War, as Freer reported to Hecker the next day: "London has gone mad this week over the peace agreement with the Boers. Last night was the first evening of jubilation and much of it centered at this hotel" (3 June 1902, FGA Hecker).

65 Telegram from Whistler to Freer

[London]
[6 June 1902]

FREER CARLTON HOTEL HAYMKT
SO SORRY IMPOSSIBLE TODAY WILL TOMORROW DO FROM
FIVE THIRTY[1]
WHISTLER

FGA Whistler 56. Post Office telegram handed in at King's Road telegraph office at 2:13 P.M., received 2:35 P.M.; stamped Charles Street, Haymarket, SW, 6 June 1902; with notation in Freer's hand, "Theobald paintings at Marchants—," referring to the collection of small pictures Freer had just purchased from Henry Studdy Theobald (1847–1934), a prominent London attorney.

---

1. According to Freer's pocket diary, Whistler and Rosalind Philip dined with him at the Carlton hotel on 7 June.

66 Letter from Rosalind Philip to Freer

74 Cheyne Walk,
Chelsea, S.W.,
June 12th, 1902.

Dear Mr. Freer:

I enclose the "little note" which you asked for.[1] I do not know if the account with the "Company of the Butterfly" is correct but you will no doubt have a list somewhere of what you received from them.

With kindest regards,

Yours very sincerely,
Rosalind Birnie Philip

[enclosure]
Company of the Butterfly.

					£.s.d.
March	1900	Lithographs.[2]	"Needlework"[3]	1 proof	4.4.0
"	"	"	"Father & Son"	" "	4.4.0
"	"	"	"Savoy Pigeons"	" "	4.4.0
May	"	1 Water colour.	"Chelsea Children"[4]		73.10.0
"	"	Lithograph	"Study of a Horse"		5.5.0
May	1902	Etchings	"The Garden"	1 proof	12.12.0
"	"	"	"The Bead Stringers"	" "	8.8.0
"	"	2 Pastels	——————	@ 150 ges. each	315.0.0
"	"	Oil painting.	Marine[5]	@ 250 ges.	262.10.0
"	"	"	"Little Lady Sophie"[6]	@ 800 ges.	840.0.0
"	"	"	"La Cigale"[7]	@ 400 ges.	420.0.0
"	"	"	"Phryne"[8]	@ 600 ges.	630.0.0

	2579.17.0
Received on account	1050.0.0
	£1529.17.0

Typescript of letter, FGA Philip; account, FGA Whistleriana 276. Notation on letter in Freer's hand, "Gave list to Mr. Whistler for correction, also draft for 2,000 pounds," and on enclosed account, "Not used—see a/c in my handwriting."

---

1. Freer wrote to Hecker on 30 May asking Hecker to send him more money as there was a chance of getting his account with Whistler settled and he wanted to be "prepared with adequate and ready funds"; he wrote again on 3 June that he and Whistler had set aside the following day "as a day to ourselves, when I hope to get from him a statement of account. But one can never tell what to expect from him in the way of figures" (FGA Hecker).

2. Details of the prints Freer purchased from the Company of the Butterfly in 1900 and from Whistler in 1902 are given in appendix B.

3. *Needlework* (W113), fig. 41.

4. *Chelsea Children*, plate 13.

5. Freer had purchased *Grey and Silver: Pourville* (present whereabouts unknown) on behalf of William K. Bixby, who had long wanted "an important example" of Whistler's work (Freer to W. S. Marchant, 19 December 1901, FGA Letterpress Book 8). It was, Freer advised Bixby, "a beautiful little picture and in [Whistler's] very best later method" (26 August 1902, FGA Letterpress Book 9).

6. *Rose and Gold: The Little Lady Sophie of Soho,* plate 12.

7. *Rose and Brown: La Cigale,* plate 11.

8. *Purple and Gold: Phryne the Superb!—Builder of Temples,* fig. 9.

67 Amended account from Freer to Whistler

Carlton Hotel, Pall Mall,
London.
[16] June, 1902.

Memorandum from Mr Whistler to C. L. Freer.
Company of the Butterfly

1900					£.s.d.
March	Lithographs[1]	"Needlework"[2]	1 proof	$21.00	4.4.0
	"	"Father & Son"	1 "	21.00	4.4.0
	"	"Savoy Pigeons"	1 "	21.00	4.4.0
May	1 Water color	"Chelsea Children"[3]		367.50	73.10.0
"	Lithograph	"Study of a Horse"	1 proof	26.25	5.5.0
"	Etching	"The Terrace Luxembourg"[4]	1 proof	63.00	12.12.0
"	"	"Cafe Luxembourg"		42.00	8.8.0

1902					
May	Etching	"The Garden"	1 proof	63.00	12.12.0
"	"	"The Bead Stringers"	1 "	42.00	8.8.0
"	Oil Painting	Marine, "Gray & Silver, Trouville" for WK Bixby,[5] Esq.	250 ges=		262.10.0
"	Pastel.	A young girl seated on a sofa holding a doll. "The Violet Cap."[6]			
"	"	A woman sitting in a chair holding a baby[7]	Each 150 ges=		315.0.0
"	"Oil Painting[8]	"Little Lady Sophie"	800 ges=		840.0.0
"	" "	"La Cigale"	400 "=		420.0.0
"	" "	"Phryne"	600 "=		630.0.0
"	Pastel	Standing female writing on the wall[9]			
"	"	A woman lying on a sofa[10]	Ea 150 ges =		315.0.0
					£2.915.17.0
Paid by Mr Freer October 1894			£1050		
" " " " June 1902			£2000		3.050.0.0
	Amount due from Mr Whistler[11]				£134.3.0

In progress for Mr Freer.	Unpaid.[12]
"The Little Blue Girl."	"
"The Little Red Glove."	"
Portrait of Mr Freer	"

[notation in Whistler's hand]

O.K.

J. McNeill Whistler

FGA Whistleriana 276. Hotel letterhead. Notations in another hand, "w180" (before "The Garden") and "w164" (before "The Bead Stringers"). Freer noted dollar amounts in red ink.

---

1. Details of the prints Freer purchased from the Company of the Butterfly in 1900 and from Whistler in 1902 are given in appendix B.

2. *Needlework* (w113), fig. 41.

3. *Chelsea Children,* plate 13.

4. *Balustrade, Luxembourg Gardens* (k427), fig. 34.

5. *Grey and Silver: Pourville* (present whereabouts unknown).

6. The pastel Freer describes is *The Green Cap,* fig. 42.

7. *The Purple Cap,* fig. 43.

8. The oil paintings Freer refers to are *Rose and Gold: The Little Lady Sophie of Soho,* plate 12, *Rose and Brown: La Cigale,* plate 11, and *Purple and Gold: Phryne the Superb!—Builder of Temples,* fig. 9.

9. *Writing on the Wall,* fig. 40.

10. *Sleeping,* 02.114. In a "Memorandum of Payments Made to J. McNeill Whistler, June 16th, 1902," dated 25 August 1902, Freer noted that the pastel showing a girl "seated on a sofa," *The Green Cap,* fig. 42, and the standing female figure, *Writing on the Wall,* fig. 40, remained with Whistler for further work; the "woman lying on a sofa," or *Sleeping,* was left for Whistler "to add some orange." *Purple and Gold: Phryne the Superb!—Builder of Temples,* fig. 9, was on exhibition in Paris (at the Société Nationale des Beaux-Arts in the Grand Palais), "from where it was sent back to Mr. Whistler's Studio—it still remains there" (FGA Art Inventories/Whistler/Misc.).

11. In his August memorandum Freer defined this as the amount he had overpaid Whistler, "to be deducted from some future settlement."

12. Although Freer had paid Whistler 1,000 guineas for *Harmony in Blue and Gold: The Little Blue Girl,* plate 2, in 1894, he credited £1,050 to his account, which meant that he still owed Whistler for the picture; he offered 1,500 guineas. No price had previously been set for the other two oils, *Portrait of Charles Lang Freer,* plate 5, and *The Little Red Glove,* 03.180, one of a series of portraits Whistler painted of Lillie Pamington, whom he met in the streets near his Fitzroy Street studio. Freer received all three paintings in 1903. See "Memorandum of paintings belonging to C. L. Freer left with Mr. Whistler," 18 June 1902, FGA Art Inventories/Whistler/Misc.

Fig. 42. *The Green Cap,* 1890s–1902. Pastel on brown paper (18.1 x 27.6), 02.112.

Fig. 43. *The Purple Cap,* 1890s. Pastel on brown paper (27.6 x 18.1), 02.111.

68 Telegram from Whistler to Freer

B SGRAVENHAGE¹ 54 29
31 12H46 S
[31 July 1902]

= MORE GOOD LUCK AFFECTIONATE MESSAGES FROM ALL
WIRE ARRIVAL WHISTLER BEAUTIFUL BUTTERFLIES JUST CAME
WORTHY DAGE AND DAIMIS ALL ENCHANTED = WHISTLER

FGA Whistler 58. Delivered to Freer at Stateroom E, *Ryndham* BSM; stamped
Pas de Calais, 31 July 1902; with notations in Freer's hand, "Doge" (below
"DAGE") and "Daimyo" (below "DAIMIS").

---

1. 'S Gravenhage (The Hague), the Netherlands. Freer spent several weeks
with Whistler and Rosalind Philip in The Hague after Whistler suffered a
heart attack en route to Amsterdam. He attempted to depart on 31 July but
missed his boat (see letter 69); Whistler's telegram was returned, then sent to
Anvers, or Antwerp, Belgium, where Freer was awaiting the next ship bound
for America (see letters 72 and 73).

6.9 Letter from Freer to Whistler

Hôtel St.-Antoine
Anvers [Belgium]
August 1 1902

Dear Mr. Whistler:—

When you start for America next fall, as I hope you will, beware of the steamship agents and porters at The Hague.

With childish confidence I trusted them, followed their directions, and of course, "got left"—on the dock at Rotterdam, looking seaward with the good ship "Ryndam" in the middle distance spurting for America. At The Hague the stupid fools had told me that the steamer would not sail until 10.30 and that I should not start from there until 8.00—

However, she did and always does sail promptly at 9.30 and I should have started one hour earlier.

Served me right! Why depend upon the brains of such people?—it is bad enough to make use of their hands and feet!

Well, it was rather shocking to be so near and yet so far. I did not need even Miss Birnie-Philip's good eyes to see a pretty ship and lots of fine looking people on board.

The Manager of the line extended all sorts of sympathy, voluntarily refunded my money and said wicked words to his agent at The Hague over the wire.

Rotterdam was too gloomy and dirty for even an hours stay, so I paddled through the mud to a pleasant river steamer and sailed to Dordrecht instead of America. At Dordrecht I found a good luncheon, pretty river views, a fine old church, and one of the best looking old one-storey houses I have ever seen! It proved to be a sufficiently quiet spot in which to exercise a little gray matter and to cool my temper, so, in due time, I continued my journey and enjoyed a good dinner and an excellent nights rest in this hotel.

It is now nearly noon and I have secured a most

comfortable room on the Red Line S.S. "Vaderland" sailing from this port tomorrow (Saturday) at noon. I have already been on board of her and am delighted with her appearance. She is due to arrive in New York on Sunday night or early Monday morning the 11th inst. The trip will be long and slow but my only objection to that will be my anxiety about my brother.[1]

But enough of all this—How are you? Gaining health and strength, I hope; and all goes well with the ladies I trust. To you all the best of all high things and much affection from

Your friend,
Charles L. Freer

GUL Whistler F462. Hotel letterhead.

---

1. Freer had planned to visit Capri after leaving The Hague but on 31 July, the day he was to depart, news of the serious illness of his elder brother, George Townsend Freer (1851–1903), called him back to the United States.

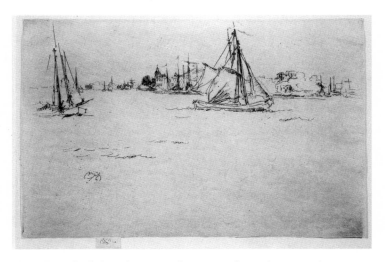

Fig. 44. *Dordrecht* (K242), 1884. Etching, second state (14.8 x 22.7), 96.46. Since the seventeenth century, artists had been drawn to the picturesque Dutch commune of Dordrecht on the River Maas.

70 Telegram from Whistler to Freer

SGRAVENHAGE 61 14
1/8 2 50
[1 August 1902]

= CANT GO THIS TIME WITHOUT OUR LETTERS = WHISTLER

FGA Whistler 59. Delivered to Freer at Hôtel St. Antoine, Anvers; stamped Anvers, 1 August 1902.

71 Telegram from Freer to Whistler

ANVERS 845 15/16 1/8
8/55 N
[1 August 1902]

CERTAINLY NOT AM WAITING PROSPECT FOR TOMORROW EXCELLENT THANKS = FREER

GUL Whistler F464. Received at 'S Gravenhage (The Hague).

30. Lange Voorhout.[1]
La Haye
Aug. 1st 1902.

Amazing! It is like some wild Opéra Bouffe! One that Offenbach had forgotten to write.[2] Still we scarcely know whether to laugh, or to cry, at all your annoyances, and our astonishments!

There certainly cannot be anything more absurd than the fact of your being so near, and yet for once really so far away.

(You see I suppose who is dictating this!)

He is very much excited and says that he is sure you will alter the whole plan of that Steam Company's life directly you get your foot on United States land—

You will be pleased to know that we have all been very miserable without you, but had settled down into a kind of jog trot sadness that would have taken you across the Atlantic, and your return is at this moment something of a shock.

We have lived with beautiful flowers, pretty last thoughts, and returned telegrams,[3] and at the present moment your ship has doubtless carried off to America two that had followed you to Boulogne.

This must go at once, as Mr Rey[4] is waiting to express it. So then again best luck and bon voyage from us all.

[in Whistler's hand]
With most affectionate messages
My dear Freer

Always devotedly
J. McNeill Whistler

[in Philip's hand]
P.S. The enclosed we thought yesterday not to send on.[5]

FGA Whistler 60 (copy, GUL Whistler LB4:38–39), with notation in Freer's hand, "ansd Aug 1st." Envelope addressed to Freer at Hôtel St. Antoine, Anvers, and inscribed, "Expressed"; stamped EXPRES; postmarked Anvers (Station), 1 August 1902, and Amsterdam-Antwerpen, 2 August 1902.

---

1. When Whistler fell ill, Ethel Philip Whibley joined Freer and Rosalind Philip in The Hague. Whistler and his sisters-in-law moved to this address, a few doors away from the Hôtel des Indes, on 26 July, when Whistler was well enough to get out of bed.

2. Jacques Offenbach (1819–1880), French musician and composer whose theater for the performance of one-act operettas, Bouffes-Parisiens, Whistler may have frequented during his student days in Paris.

3. Probably including letter 68.

4. Rey (or "Ray," as it is sometimes spelled in Freer's and Philip's correspondence) seems to have served as the party's interpreter in Holland.

5. The enclosure has not been identified.

73 Letter from Freer to Whistler

Hôtel St.-Antoine
Anvers
August 1st 1902
9 P.M.

Dear Mr. Whistler:—

Since my earlier letter of today most delightful things have happened.

Mr. Rey has telephoned and told me of your kind telegram sent to Bologne and other pleasant news. Already from him has arrived a copy of the charming message, and another of todays date, direct from yourself and the ladies is here. And now, to fill my cup of happiness comes your beautiful letter of this afternoon.[1]

As the missed ship rushed out of the harbour without me the faithful Stefano murmured mysteriously "good luck will come to you for this accident."

It is already here. But it would be still more perfect if instead of sending written thoughts I could go to you all in person as was the habit for so many evenings.

Let us see! Why not reverse the route and you and the ladies come to me? October is the best month in America. My little home is most simple and my kind of entertainment is still simpler. But if you will come and try it for a while you will be sure to find a warm welcome. Do come. And again with best wishes and affectionate regard to you all

Always faithfully
Charles L. Freer

P.S. Two ~~of the~~ ladies who crossed in the same steamer with me a year ago and who occupied seats at my table arrived here an hour ago and told me they are to sail on the same steamer with me tomorrow.[2] More good luck!

GUL Whistler F463. Hotel letterhead.

---

1. Freer probably refers to letters 68, 70, and 72, all delivered to Anvers.

2. According to Freer's pocket diary, these were Miss Miller of Albany and Miss Wright of New York.

74 Telegram from Freer to Whistler

ANTWERPEN 2215 31/32
2/8 12 57 N
[2 August 1902]

YOUR SUFFERING IS THE ONLY CLOUD THIS BRIGHT MORNING
OF SUCCESSFUL STARTING TO ALL GOOD LUCK GOOD HEALTH
MUCH HAPPINESS AND AFFECTION WILL WIRE ARRIVAL= FREER +

GUL Whistler F465. Received at 'S Gravenhage (The Hague).

75 Letter from Rosalind Philip to Freer

30 Lange Voorhout,
La Haye,
Sunday, August 3d,
1902.

Dear Mr. Freer:

I am writing to thank you very much for your kind letter which Stefano delivered quite safely. We will certainly make use of him when we have need. We were much pleased to hear that you started on your journey with everything looking hopeful for a good voyage.

Everything here is as usual, except that today Mr. Whistler is, we think, improved. The doctor[1] himself seemed pleased and you can imagine the joy of the sisters-in-law when lobster was ordered for his lunch!

Mrs. Whibley and I are bearing up and have laid in a supply of needlework before our good resolutions fail, and you may expect the masterpieces later on. There has been much consultation and the result will be something quite unique. We hope they will be properly treasured and treated with high consideration.[2]

We all miss you very much and we have talked about you a great deal, but we are shortly to be consoled. Mr. William Heinemann is looming large in the near distance. At present we are debating which of us shall assist at his reception. Mrs. Whibley stands firm for a precipitate retreat to our part of the apartment.

We would like to come and see you beyond everything, but we must not say we will, you are so far away. Rather we must look forward to your coming next year.

We all send you many affectionate messages and my sister and I shall always bear in remembrance all your great kindness to us in our troubles, which no expression of ours can tell you how much we felt.

We hope you found good news awaiting you and that all is well with you.

Always very sincerely yours,
Rosalind Birnie Philip

Typescript, FGA Philip.

---

1. Freer had written to Hecker from The Hague that Whistler's physician was "the celebrated Dr. Coert who attended the Queen [Wilhelmina (1890–1948) of the Netherlands] during her recent illness, an able and attentive doctor" (27 June 1902, FGA Hecker).

2. Rosalind Philip and Ethel Whibley were embroidering needlepoint slippers for Freer, which were to be virtually destroyed by a careless shoemaker. See Philip to Freer, 26 September 1902 and 5 December 1902, FGA Philip.

76 Cablegram from Whistler to Freer

SGRAVENHAGE 12

AUG 12 1902

FREER

KINGSTON NY[1]

GOOD US ALSO BEST AFFECTION OUT TWICE

WHISTLER.

FGA Whistler 61. Western Union Telegraph Company cable, received at 306 Wall Street, Kingston, New York; with notation in Freer's hand, "phoned."

---

1. Freer had gone directly to his brother George Freer's home in Kingston, New York, and remained there a week, until his brother's health improved (Freer to W. K. Bixby, 26 August 1902, FGA Letterpress Book 9).

77 Letter from Freer to Whistler

33 Ferry Avenue
Detroit, Michigan.
October 15th, 1902.

Dear Mr. Whistler:—

Will you kindly read the enclosed correspondence at your leisure, and let me know your pleasure in the matter? Personally, I know nothing of the lady.[1]

I am just home again from a three weeks driving trip through the White mountains and Berkshire hills, and am in fine fettle to meet the extremes of our American winter. How are you? much better I hope.

During my late travels I accidently met Mr. Canfield who seemed very well, and very enthusiastic over the recent purchase of one of your masterpieces.[2] He is a lucky man.

With affectionate regards and all good wishes,

Yours very sincerely,
Charles L. Freer

GUL Whistler F468. Personal stationery.

---

1. Nancy R. E. Meugens Bell to Freer, 18 September 1902 (GUL Whistler B46), and Freer to Bell, 14 October 1902 (FGA Letterpress Book 9; copy, GUL Whistler F467). Bell (d. 1933) wrote to ask permission to reproduce some paintings in Freer's collection. Freer replied that it was his "invariable rule" to refer such requests to the artists themselves and advised her to write to Whistler directly.

2. Richard A. Canfield (1855–1914) was an art collector and proprietor of casinos in New York, Saratoga, and Newport. He purchased *Arrangement in Black and Gold: Comte Robert de Montesquiou-Fezensac* (Frick Collection, New York) from the French poet Montesquiou (1855–1921) through the Paris dealer André J. Seligman. Montesquiou had met Whistler through Henry James (1843–1916) in 1885 and introduced him into Parisian society. Whistler was deeply offended when he learned, through Canfield, that his friend had sold the portrait. Whistler's lithograph, *Count Robert de Montesquiou, No. 2* (W138), is shown in fig. 45.

Fig. 45. *Count Robert de Montesquiou, No. 2* (W138), 1894–95. Lithograph (21.3 x 9.5), 03.215. Signed in pencil with the butterfly. Whistler intended to publish a lithograph after his oil portrait of Montesquiou in the *Gazette des Beaux-Arts* and produced several ultimately unsatisfactory versions. He wrote to his printer T. R. Way in despair, saying that his drawing was "no more like the superb original than if it had been done by my worst and most competent enemy!" (15 July 1894, FGA Way).

78 Whistler's calling card, inscribed to Freer

[London]

[31 December 1902]

To Charles L. Freer, with MR. J. MCNEILL WHISTLERS affectionate messages, & best wishes for 1903.

FGA Whistler 43-c. Card (mourning), imprinted, "Mr. J. McNeill Whistler, / Cheyne Walk, Chelsea. / 110, Rue du Bac." Probably sent in envelope (FGA Whistler 43) addressed to Freer at 33 Ferry Avenue, Detroit; postmarked Chelsea, 31 December 1902, and Detroit, 14 January 1903.

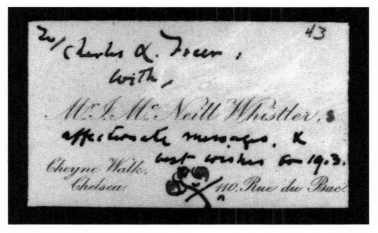

Fig. 46. Whistler's calling card.

79 Letter from Freer to Whistler

No. 33 Ferry Ave.,
Detroit, Mich.
Mar. 30th, 1903.

Dear Mr. Whistler:—

You doubtless have heard, ere this, through my several letters to Mr. Canfield of the particulars leading up to the agreement under which I was to furnish three examples of your Paintings, to the Exhibition of the Society of American Artists, now being held in New York.[1]

The original request came to me from Mr. Will H. Low, a member of the Soliciting Committee of the Society:[2] After consulting with Mr. Canfield and acting under authority from him, I promised the Portrait of "Count Robert." Later I was requested by Mr. Canfield from London to withdraw the "Count Robert" which I did.

After Mr. Canfield had purchased the "Rosa Corder" he informed me that if I cared to do so, I might loan the picture to the Society, and suggested that I add something of your work, from my own collection.

I communicated with Mr. Low, promptly, and told him that a Friend of mine, the owner of "Count Robert," had recently purchased the lovely "Rosa Corder" and that he had generously authorized me to loan her to the forthcoming exhibition and that I would cheerfully send additional works by you from my own collection, provided the Society really desired them, and would willingly hang them in one group in a place of honor. I also said to Mr. Low that in naming the matter to the Board of Control, he might, if he chose to do, say that you had cheerfully consented to the Exhibition, also that you sent your Compliments and Greetings to the Society.

Being in a generous mood I further said to Mr. Low that

as he had seen my collection of your work, and had named his favorites, he might, if he wished, select therefrom examples to hang with the "Rosa Corder." We discussed the matter fully and he finally decided that his choice would be the "Nocturne Blue and Silver Battersea Reach,"[3] formerly owned by Mr. Rawlinson and the "Nocturne Grey and Silver, Chelsea Embankment, Winter," formerly owned by Mr. Orchar. In this way the group was determined and the agreement made.

Fig. 47. *Nocturne: Grey and Silver—Chelsea Embankment, Winter,* 1879. Oil on canvas (62.6 x 47.5), 02.143.

Also the time of the arrival of the "Rosa Corder" was discussed, which I feared even at that time, might be somewhat delayed by the Red Tape methods of Custom House Officials, and allowance for possible delay was accordingly made. A few days thereafter I visited Philadelphia to see the Exhibition of the Philadelphia Academy,[4] and finding your work not as well hung as I had expected from my correspondence with Mr. Morris, notwithstanding that it was the last day of the Exhibition, I went directly to him and entered a vigorous verbal protest. At first he insisted that the place given to your pictures was as good as any in the Galleries, which I turned and pointed out to him that the place of honor was given to Mr. Sargent's Portrait of Mr. Chase, that a fine center was given to Mr. Alexander's weak work etc. etc.,[5] all of which led to much talk about Hanging Committees, their treatment of specially invited pictures etc.

With this disappointment stirring my blood, I returned to New York and went early the next morning direct to Mr. Low's Studio, told him how unfairly your pictures had been treated in Philadelphia, and asked if in his opinion anything of the same sort was likely to happen in New York. He said, "Certainly not," but suggested that there might spring up a desire on the part of the Hanging Committee, to give the first place of honor, (there are two places of honor in the Vanderbilt Gallery equally good) to Sargent's Portrait of President Roosevelt,[6] to which I replied, "Certainly any portrait of the President of the United States, which would pass the Jury, no matter by whom painted, should be given the first place of honor, let it have the center of the North Wall and give Mr. Whistler the center of the East Wall." All of which was agreed to and I, thinking everything perfectly arranged, returned to Detroit.

The Sargent Portrait of President Roosevelt, for reasons unknown to me, was not sent to the Society although I supposed it had been, until I reached New York a few days ago.

Later a letter came from Mr. Low to me here, enclosing one written by Mr. Kenyon Cox,[7] Chairman of Soliciting Committee, to Mr. Low, in which he spoke of the expense of transportation and insurance of your pictures and expressed some anxiety about the financial affairs of the Society, and as I then wrongly fancied, said between the lines that Cox, not Low, should have invited the Whistlers and arranged matters with Freer.

Since then I have learned that Cox is one of your staunchest admirers and that he, more ably than any other man, argued before the Board of Control not to let me have your pictures back when I demanded them, but to put them where they so justly belonged, in the place of honor. But, as said before, when reading Cox's letter to Low, I fancied that I saw jealously between the lines, so in order to anticipate any trouble about money, I immediately telegraphed that I would gladly pay all expenses myself, and wrote Mr. Low that I was very much inclined to then withdraw the pictures, fearing some obstacle to their proper honor might be instigated by Cox. To this letter of mine, I received a letter from Low, telling me that I misjudged Cox, that Low should not have sent me Cox's letter, that everything was running smoothly and that a special meeting of the Society would be called at once to thank Mr. Whistler, to thank Mr. Freer, and to assure us both that the pictures should be hung as agreed.

In due time the letter of thanks came, containing the statement "that the pictures should be hung together in one of the most honorable positions in the galleries," which naturally, to my mind, confirmed the conversation had with Mr. Low about the center of the north or east walls, which are of course the places of honor, not only in the mind of the public, but in the mind of Mr. Low and the Board of Control and the Hanging Committee as well, all of which is so frankly admitted in the telegram of the Secretary of the Society to me, dated March 20th, reading: "an important position was reserved" and "there are only two more honorable places than this in the Gallery."[8]

Please notice, however, that in the letter of the Society of March 24th, written in the evening and sent by special messenger at ten o'clock to my hotel, after the Editorial in the afternoon edition of the New York Sun had defended my course, and explained the rights of lenders of invited pictures,[9] the Society tries to imply that the Board of Control in telegraphing me, had no knowledge of Mr. Low's verbal promise, nor no intention to confirm the same. If I cared for a controversy or a fight through the Newspapers, it would be simple enough to convince the Public, by letting Mr. Low tell his side of the story and publishing the correspondence, but for such business I have neither time nor taste, and have advised silence on the part of Mr. Low. Why advertise the Society's Exhibition by carelessly using your name?

Copies of the correspondence between the Society and myself are enclosed herein, which will explain fully to you the circumstances of the withdrawal of your pictures. In order to give you all of the facts, it only remains for me to add that while in New York during last week, I refrained from talking with the Newspapers and the Members of the Society, excepting only Mr. Low, and its President, Mr. John La Farge,[10] although a great many people attempted to interview me, or to drag me into the clutches of the Press. Mr. La Farge called upon me in person to deliver the letter of which I enclose a copy, but I was out at the time: He repeated his call, but again unfortunately I was out. Then I made an engagement and called upon him: He discussed the unfortunate affair with real personal feeling and regret. He is extremely sorry to lose the pictures for the Exhibition and particularly distressed at the thought that you may feel that an injustice has been done your work. He consented to my suggestion that his letter to me herewith enclosed, be sent to you, and he said that he felt it a duty to write to you personally, to explain the real feeling of highest respect entertained for you and your work by the Society of American Artists, as a body.

I advised him to do so, and you will hear directly from him by early mail. I would have written you earlier but for the fact that I wanted to give you the whole story complete in itself and the fullest knowledge could only be obtained by a personal visit to New York. I have cabled and written about the matter to Mr. Canfield, as progress was made, and he has of course, from time to time, kept you informed. In a cablegram received from Mr. Canfield some days ago, he said that both you and he fully approved of my action: For your joint support and approval, I am deeply grateful.

In caring for such of your work as has fallen into my fortunate hands, I have, and always shall, treat it to the fullest extent in the same dignified manner, that I believe you, yourself, would exercise, or expect others to exercise in your behalf. If, in the present instance, you should find, with the facts all before you, any omission or commission on my part, which you would have wished differently done, I beg you to tell me frankly for my future guidance.

I do hope that you are gaining health and strength daily and that you are enjoying life and your work as of old. I am very well, in a rush of business, and other affairs preparatory to beginning my summer tour, which is scheduled to start on April 14th, from New York, via S.S. "Liguria" for Capri, after Capri, Spain, Paris and London. At the latter place I hope to see you and to find you in the fullest enjoyment of your old time strength, and interest in all things worth while.

Shall you be in Chelsea after June 15th? and if you are in the mood would you be willing to resume work on my Portrait?[11]

> With affectionate greetings to all,
> [Charles L. Freer]

Typescript copy, FGA Society of American Artists.

---

1. Twenty-fifth Annual Exhibition of the Society of American Artists, Fine Arts Building, New York, which opened on 27 March 1903. Freer provided two of Canfield's paintings, *Arrangement in Black and Gold: Comte Robert de Montesquiou-Fezensac* (Frick Collection, New York) and *Arrangement in Brown and Black: Portrait of Miss Rosa Corder* (Frick Collection, New York), which Canfield had purchased from W. Graham Robertson in February 1903. He also lent *Nocturne: Grey and Silver—Chelsea Embankment, Winter*, fig. 47, which he had purchased the previous year from G. N. Stevens of Virginia Water, England; its previous owner had been J. G. Orchar (d. 1898) of Dundee, Scotland.

2. Will H. Low (1853–1932), mural painter, designer, and illustrator. The purpose of the Soliciting Committee was to borrow works for the annual exhibition from outside the society's membership.

3. *Nocturne: Blue and Silver—Battersea Reach,* plate 16.

4. Seventy-second Annual Exhibition of the Pennsylvania Academy of the Fine Arts, Philadelphia, 19 January–28 February 1903. Freer lent five works by Whistler: *Blue and Gold—The Rose Azalea,* plate 8, *Rose and Red: The Little Pink Cap,* plate 9, *Rose and Brown: La Cigale,* plate 11, *Rose and Gold:*

The Little Lady Sophie of Soho, plate 12, and *Violet and Silver: The Great Sea,* then titled "Green and Gold—The Great Sea," 02.148.

5. *William Merritt Chase, N.A.* (Metropolitan Museum of Art, New York) was painted by John Singer Sargent (1856–1925) in July 1902, while the artist William Merritt Chase (1849–1916) was in London with his friend Harrison S. Morris (1856–1948), managing director of the Pennsylvania Academy of the Fine Arts. John White Alexander (1856–1915), born in Pennsylvania, was a leading portrait and mural painter and a friend of Whistler's.

6. Sargent, *Portrait of Theodore Roosevelt* (The White House, Washington, D.C.), 1902.

7. Kenyon Cox (1856–1919), American mural painter and illustrator.

8. Freer sent the telegram from Henry Prellwitz to Whistler but retained a copy, which is filed in the FGA Archives with other correspondence pertaining to the 1903 Society of American Artists' exhibition. The place of honor on the north wall of the Vanderbilt room was occupied by a painting by Abbott Handerson Thayer (1849–1921), *Stevenson Memorial* (National Museum of American Art, Smithsonian Institution), 1903; Sargent's portrait of Chase hung in the center of the east wall.

9. "Mr. Freer, Mr. Will Low and the Society," *New York Evening Sun,* 24 March 1903, FGA Whistler Scrapbook 1:3: "The present situation, as far as we can judge, is the result of a certain carelessness that seems to be singularly prevalent among the borrowers of pictures . . . . The borrowers apparently think that, having secured the desired objects, they are under no further obligation to the lenders. Is it any wonder that some of our collectors are unwilling to let the public share their enjoyments, when the go-betweens are so indifferent?"

10. John La Farge (1835–1910), American painter and designer.

11. *Portrait of Charles Lang Freer,* plate 5.

80 Cablegram from Whistler to Freer

LONDON
MAR 31ST. 03
281CH Y R 17 3:05.P.M.

FREER.,
DETROIT.
AM DELIGHTED MOST RAPID AND BRILLIANT ACTION COULD
NOT HAVE BEEN IN BETTER HANDS
WHISTLER

FGA Whistler 62. Postal Telegraph-Cable Company cablegram.

81 Letter from Freer to Whistler

33 Ferry Avenue
Detroit, Michigan
April 3rd, 1903.

Dear Mr. Whistler;

Your cordial telegram assuring me of your approval of
my action in withdrawing your paintings from the current
exhibition of the Society of American Artists gives me much
pleasure.

It is a real delight to feel that your wishes were anticipated and promptly executed.

All of the leading American newspapers have condemned
the bad management of the three ~~leading~~ official divisions
of the Society—i.e. the board of control, the jury and the
hanging committee. The newspapers and the public express

much disappointment at the loss of an opportunity to see your work.

I accidentally met Mr. Knoedler[1] while in New York recently, and exchanged a few words with him on the subject, which of course was then the topic of conversation in art circles. In parting he said "whenever Mr. Whistler wishes to exhibit his work in New York, my galleries are at his disposal."

I might add, that I am confident without having raised the question, that the same can safely be said of every other first class public gallery in all America. Galleries are numerous enough, but the rub comes when one tries to get examples of your work.

Mr. Canfield has been most thoughtful and supporting in our first round with the Society, and what is still more important, he tells us of your increasing strength. Wishing you perfect health, I am, with affectionate greetings,

Charles L. Freer

GUL Whistler F470. Personal stationery.

---

1. Of M. Knoedler & Co., successors to Goupil & Co. in New York.

82 Letter from Freer to Whistler

Dal bordo del
piroscafo "Liguria"
24th April, 1903.

Dear Mr. Whistler;

Some time ago an admirer of your work, Mr. Bunkio Matsuki,[1] of Japan and Boston, handed me some sheets of ancient Japanese paper, and requested me to send them to you with his compliments and the hope that they might be of some use to you in your art.

The paper was put away at my home, with the intention of sending the same to you at a more convenient moment, and eventually was forgotten.

It was rescued from its safe hiding place the day of my recent start for Italy, and I ordered it forwarded from my office to you by American Express.

I hope that the paper will reach you in good order and that it may interest you.

I am making the approach to sunny Italy in appropriate manner—on board a steamer "very Italian" with every body, including myself, sea sick.

You are very well, I trust.

Always affectionately yours
Charles L. Freer

GUL Whistler F472. Navigazione Generale Italiana letterhead.

---

1. Matsuki Bunkyō (1867–1940) was a Japanese art dealer Freer had known since 1896. Freer gave Matsuki a card of introduction to Whistler on 27 July 1897 (FGA Letterpress Book 4).

83 Telegram from Whistler to Freer

[London]
[16 June 1903]

CHARLES FREER CARLTON HOTEL HAYMARKET
ARE YOU THERE EXPECTED YOUR APPEARANCE BY NOW[1]
AFFECTIONATE GREETINGS
WHISTLER

FGA Whistler 63. Post Office telegram handed in at King's Road telegraph office at 7:54 P.M., received 8:20 P.M.; stamped West Strand, WC, 16 June 1903.

1. Freer was in Burgos, Spain; he went to Paris the next day and to London on 30 June 1903.

84 Telegram from Whistler to Freer

[London]
[30 June 1903]

CHARLES FREER HOTEL CECIL LONDON
DELIGHTED TO SEE YOU THIS AFTERNOON AT ABOUT FOUR
WHISTLER

FGA Whistler 64. Post Office telegram handed in at King's Road telegraph office at 1:20 [P.M.], received 1:41 [P.M.]; stamped Strand, WC, 30 June 1903.

85 Letter from Rosalind Philip to Freer

74 Cheyne Walk,
Chelsea,
July 2d, 1903.

Dear Mr. Freer:

Knowing that you will be anxious to hear how Mr.
Whistler is, I am happy to say he is a little better today.
He wishes me to thank you for the very beautiful flowers.
With kindest regards,

Yours very sincerely,
Rosalind Birnie Philip

Typescript, FGA Philip.

86 Telegram from Whistler to Freer

[London]
[3 July 1903]

CHARLES FREER
COBURG HOTEL GROSVENOR SQ.
ARE YOU COMING TO SEE ME THIS AFTERNOON
WHISTLER

FGA Whistler 65. Post Office telegram handed in at King's Road telegraph
office at 2:55 P.M., received 3:17 P.M.; stamped South Audley Street, 3 July 1903.

87 Telegram from Whistler to Freer

[London]
[4 July 1903]

CHARLES FREER COBURG HOTEL GROSVENOR SQ
BE SURE COME AND SEE US TOMORROW WIRE WHEN TO
EXPECT YOU
WHISTLER

FGA Whistler 66. Post Office telegram handed in at King's Road telegraph office at 7:23 P.M., received 7:53 P.M.; stamped South Audley Street, 4 July 1903; with notation in Freer's hand, "5 P.M."

88 Telegram from Whistler to Freer

[London]
[6 July 1903]

CHARLES FREER COBURG HOTEL GROS SQRE
COME DOWN WITHOUT FAIL TO DRIVE OUT WITH ME AT
THREE THIS AFTERNOON
WHISTLER

FGA Whistler 67. Post Office telegram handed in at King's Road telegraph office at 12:25 P.M., received 12:45 P.M.; stamped South Audley Street, 6 July 1903.

89 Telegram from Whistler to Freer

[London]
[15 July 1903]

CHARLES FREER
COBURG HOTEL GROSVENOR SQ
MAY GO OUT WILL YOU COME AT 3.30
WHISTLER[1]

FGA Whistler 68. Post Office telegram handed in at Sloane Square telegraph office at 11:49 A.M., received 11:55 A.M.; stamped South Audley Street, 15 July 1903.

---

1. Freer visited Whistler that afternoon, as he had virtually every day since arriving in London. Whistler died on 17 July.

Appendix A

The following article, reprinted in its entirety and without correction, was published in the *Detroit Free Press* on 30 March 1890 (FGA Whistler Scrapbook 1:2). In letter 1, Freer discusses the article and mentions that he is sending Whistler a copy.

A Day with Whistler.

C. L. Freer Tells of His Recent Visit to "Tower House."
The American Artist in London,
His Characteristics and His Home and Studio.

Just why it is that James MacNeal Whistler, the great American artist, is a man so difficult to reach either socially or in a business way, is not of as much interest as is the fact that when once one reaches him the visitor soon finds out whether or not he or she has made a favorable impression upon the man who is beyond question the most notable American-born resident of London. In view of this fact a recent experience of C. L. Freer, of this city, has in its details especial local interest.

Mr. Freer has just returned from a three weeks' tour to Europe, spending sixteen days on board ship and five days in London. Going to the world's metropolis on business the transaction of which required but four days, and being an ardent admirer of Mr. Whistler's greatness as an artist—at the same time having a day to spare before the sailing of his ship—Mr. Freer decided to devote the spare day, if need be, to obtaining an audience with the artist. How he succeeded was most interestingly related to a representative of THE FREE PRESS, substantially as follows:

"I boarded the underground and after a brief ride was set down at Sloane's Square, having been told that Mr. Whistler lived in Tite street in that vicinity. Having had a good deal of riding and but little exercise just then, I decided to walk to Tite street and so started down King's Road. After walking two or three squares I inquired of a policeman the way to Tite street, and he replied: 'Right on down King's Road.' Making the inquiry three or four times of as many different policemen as I walked on and receiving the same reply in each instance, I thought I would vary the question by asking as to the residence of Mr. Whistler. Three or four policemen were approached with this question, and in each case 'Cawn't tell,' as the answer. As I estimated that I has walked fully a mile from Sloane's Square I entered a jewelry store and asked to be told where Mr. Whistler, the artist, lived. 'Cawnt tell,' again came the answer and the same result followed a like inquiry at a fish shop. I began to feel annoyed and just then, having reached Church street, I adopted new tactics by asking a cabman if he knew where Mr. Whistler lived. 'O, yes,' he replied, 'Mr. Whistler, the artist. You go down one square and turn to the right and there you are. There's Tower House. Fine fellow is Mr. Whistler, we all knows 'im.' Then I realized that my mistake had been made in not asking the first cabman I saw at Sloane's Square."

"Presently I was at the door of Tower House and soon in answer to my summons a young man invited me to enter. When I had made known my wish to see Mr. Whistler the young man, taking my card, invited me to be seated while he ascertained as to whether or not the artist could be seen. I had had just time to note that the apartment into which I had been ushered was decorated in one of those delightful color schemes, plain and unassuming but wholly harmonious, when my usher announced that Mr. Whistler would see me in fifteen minutes. The announcement was so exact that unconsciously I consulted my watch and so to speak, I 'held my watch on him.' Promptly, the door opened and stepping quickly toward me, his white lock standing conspicuously up from the top of his head, he greeted me and asked my business. 'I understand that you are an artist,' I said to him, 'and I wanted to meet you.' After he had said 'Ah,' in a satirical sort of way, I continued, 'And I have been told that you once made an etching, and I want to see that.' The gentleman looked at me quizzically as he answered, 'What's it all about?' I replied that I was an admirer of the art of etching and that I had come all the way from Detroit to see him and being, like himself, an American, I expected to see him."

"Whether it was my assurance or that I happened to catch him in good humor, I do not know, but straightway he invited me into an adjoining room which was something of a curiosity. It was a large apartment finished in yellows, and in its center stood a long table. One end of the table was laid as though for a dinner. The middle third of the table was fitted out as a woman's sewing table and appeared to have been but recently abandoned by the worker, while the other third of the table was an artist's work shop, and was covered with sketches, paint brushes and pots, colors, etc. Here we took seats and for perhaps an hour we chatted, Mr. Whistler showing deep interest in the progress of art in America, and a remarkable knowledge of American artists, literature and general progress and bestowing many warm words of praise upon such American artists as Wm. M. Chase, F. S. Church and others. In speaking of the fact that he had been charged with having lost his interest in America, and that he was more Englishman than American, he said it was not true, but that he felt in no hurry to force himself on this side of the water; that when he went to London, alone and a stranger, having convictions and willing to stand or fall by them, as an artist, the American press not only abandoned him to his single handed fight with Turner and others, but many of the most influential of American periodicals and newspapers assailed him cruelly. Now that he had won whatever fame was his, and was in a condition to be able to do so, he was contented to rest without making advances. Then he showed me some of the most remarkable scrap-books I have ever seen. In those scrap-books, elaborately classified and indexed, he had hundreds upon hundreds of clippings from American magazines and newspapers, all dated and credited, and forming, in brief, an epitome of American press sentiment as to himself from a time away before he became prominent in London and the art world in general down to the present. It was during this conversation that I was impressed, became saturated as it were, by the man's personality and originality. A picturesque figure, full of vitality and energy, with a keen, nervous temperament, and yet with absolute control of himself, and a wonderful conversationalist, he could not fail to impress any one with his greatness."

"Presently he invited me to his studio. There I found a large apartment having high walls and a gallery. It was the ideal of an etcher's workshop, with its tables, baths, and presses, and while it had none of the typical disorder and queer embellishment of most artist's studios, it was attractive, homey and restful, at the same time being a perfect dream of harmony in its appointments. You have doubtless heard of Oscar Wilde's remark at a dinner, where, after Whistler had made one of his inimitable speeches, Mr. Wilde said, complimenting Mr. Whistler, 'I wish I had said it.' The artist replied, patronizingly,

'Never mind, Oscar, you will.' I heard another story while at the etchings exhibition in London, which serves equally well to illustrate Whistler's wit. A young lady who had been a worshiper of the artist's skill met him at a reception, and telling him of an early morning walk she had indulged in that day she gave an elaborate description of the beauty of the landscape she had seen. Then as a finale she added that then, for the first time, she realized how near Nature was to some of his pictures. 'Ah,' said Mr. Whistler, in reply, 'so Nature is catching up, is she?'"

"I only tell this to show you that which is true, that Mr. Whistler, in spite of his eccentricities, is really a cordial, big-hearted, jolly man, with a keen sense of humor; and, it is well known that no man in London is in greater demand at dinners and club affairs. By the way, Mr. James Barr, the London representative of THE FREE PRESS, who was very hospitable to me, took me, one evening, down to the Smoking Club, an organization of London journalists, musicians, actors and artists, and there I learned that Mr. Whistler is a frequent and welcome visitor. When I told Mr. Whistler of that experience and that THE FREE PRESS representative was my host, he said: 'THE FREE PRESS? Oh, yes. That is that clever American paper. Dammit (that concentration of two words is one of Mr. Whistler's favorite ejaculations), do you know that paper was a revelation of doing American things in an American way, not only to London newspapers, but to London business men?'"

"To show the position occupied, socially, by Mr. Whistler, I must tell you of an incident which came under my observation. I was standing in the corridor at the Fine Art Society's rooms talking with the secretary, when an elaborate equipage stopped in front of the gallery, and as the footman opened the carriage door a pompous man alighted. Entering the corridor he stopped and purchased a catalogue. Then coming directly to the secretary with whom I was still talking, he said: 'Beg pardon, is Mr. Whistler in?' The secretary answering in the negative, the big man continued: 'So sorry, so sorry; but will you be so good as to say to 'im that I have so enjoyed his water colors?'"

"'But you have not seen them yet,' rejoined the secretary."

"'That don't matter, you know,' said the pompous individual as he paused apologetically, 'but if I didn't call you know he wouldn't like it, he wouldn't like it. So if you'll please say to him——.' 'Very good,' said the secretary, as he turned and resumed his chat with me by saying, 'You see, the swells are all afraid of losing favor with Mr. Whistler.' That simply illustrates one little feature in the wide aspect of the man's real eminence in the world of art. His position is unique.

With a profound knowledge of art and literature and with the personal characteristics already alluded to, he has won alone and by his own merit one of the most bitter battles in the history of art and has been awarded a place in that history which cannot be shaken. A man of strong character and an artist of wondrous versatility, yet religiously careful in his attention to all details of his art, his work increases in its peculiarly distinct individuality and is being more and more recognized and distinguished as the greatest since the days of Rembrandt. It is a healthy stimulus, this appreciation which advances with his continued progress, because, by it, artists and laymen alike and especially the younger generation of artists, receive inspiration. Whistler imitates no one. He is a law unto himself, has a reason for every line and is an absolute master of the laws of omission. He is not only the great etcher, but is the great printer of etchings, prints all of his own etchings, examines each and every proof pulled, marks upon the backs symbols which to him indicate quality and effect and often some slight change in plate or printing when next he examines the proof. Nearly all of the rising etchers of to-day in much of their best work suggest the influence of Whistler and it is to be hoped that they will continue to look to him for guidance and inspiration."

Appendix B

Prints listed in the correspondence

Titles of etchings are from Edward G. Kennedy, *The Etched Work of Whistler* (New York: The Grolier Club, 1910); dates are from Katharine A. Lochnan, *The Etchings of James McNeill Whistler* (New Haven: Yale University Press, 1984), 277–85. All impressions are signed by Whistler with the butterfly and inscribed "imp" on the tab.

Titles of lithographs are from T. R. Way, *Mr. Whistler's Lithographs: The Catalogue*, 2d ed. (London: George Bell & Sons, and New York: Wunderlich & Co., 1905); dates are from Mervyn Levy, *Whistler Lithographs: A Catalogue Raisonné* (London: Jupiter Books, 1975).

Significant variants of titles are noted in quotation marks, and dates differing from those in the sources cited above are noted in square brackets.

Etchings purchased in March 1890

The list below corresponds to the list Freer provided Whistler in letter 2, dated 28 April 1890. A list in Freer's hand of the etchings and their prices, presumably made in London, survives in the FGA Archives (Art Vouchers prior to 1893).

1. *Pierrot* (K407), 1889. Etching, fourth state, printed in brown ink on cream-colored laid paper, 06.116. Inscribed by Whistler, verso, "Selected for Chs. L. Freer," and signed with the butterfly.

2. "Long House (The Dyers)." *Long House—Dyer's—Amsterdam* (K406), 1889. Etching, intermediate state between second and third, printed in brown ink on cream-colored japan paper, 06.118. Inscribed by Whistler, verso, "Chs. L. Freer," and signed with the butterfly.

3. *Zaandam* (K416), 1889. Etching, second state, printed in brown ink on cream-colored japan paper, 06.120. Inscribed by Whistler, verso, "Chs. L. Freer," and signed with the butterfly.

4. "Steps." *Steps, Amsterdam* (K403), 1889. Etching, third state, printed in brown ink on cream-colored laid paper, 06.112. Inscribed by Whistler, verso, "Selected for Chs. L. Freer," and signed with the butterfly.

5. *The Mill* (K413), 1889. Etching, first state. Printed in brown ink on cream-colored laid paper, 06.127. Inscribed by Whistler, verso, "Chs. L. Freer / 2nd Proof pulled," and signed with the butterfly.

6. "The Square House." *Square House, Amsterdam* (K404), 1889. Etching, second state, printed in brown ink on cream-colored laid paper, 06.113. Inscribed by Whistler, verso, "Selected for Chs. L. Freer," and signed with the butterfly.

7. "The Dance House (Nocturne)." *Nocturne: Dance-House* (K408), 1889. Etching, first state, printed in brown ink on cream-colored laid paper, 06.117. Inscribed by Whistler, verso, "Chs. L. Freer," and signed with the butterfly.

8. "The Balcony." *Balcony, Amsterdam* (K405), 1889. Etching, third state, printed in brown ink on cream-colored laid paper, 06.114. Inscribed by Whistler, verso, "Chosen for Chs. L. Freer," and signed with the butterfly.

9. "The Little Drawbridge." *Little Drawbridge, Amsterdam* (K412), 1889. Etching, first state, printed in brown ink on cream-colored laid paper, 06.115. Inscribed by Whistler, verso, "Chs. L. Freer / 1st proof pulled," and signed with the butterfly.

10. "The Bridge." *Bridge, Amsterdam* (K409), 1889. Etching, second state, printed in brown ink on cream-colored laid paper, 06.119. Inscribed by Whistler, verso, "Chs. L. Freer," and signed with the butterfly.

Lithographs purchased in January 1892

The lithographs Freer received in 1892 (see letter 9, dated 29 January 1892) are difficult to identify, as no contemporary account has survived and early inventories and museum records are often unreliable; moreover, as Freer intended to give some of the impressions away (see letter 7), there is no way to know with certainty which ones or how many he kept for himself. The list below includes lithographs that may have been included in the 1892 lot. All are of the right period and printed on what Whistler referred to as "Dutch and Japanese" papers; all but two are unsigned.

Gaiety Stage Door (W10), 1879. Lithograph printed in black ink on antique, tan laid paper, 88.23.

Victoria Club (W11), 1879. Lithograph printed in black ink on antique, tan laid paper, 88.26.

Old Battersea Bridge (w12), 1879. Lithograph printed in black ink on antique, tan laid paper, 88.27.

Reading (w13), 1879. Lithograph printed in black ink on antique, cream-colored laid paper, 88.29.

Entrance Gate (w16), 1887. Lithograph printed in black ink on antique, cream-colored laid paper, 06.137.

Churchyard (w17), 1887. Lithograph printed in black ink on antique, tan laid paper, 06.139.

Little Court, Cloth Fair (w18), 1887. Lithograph printed in black ink on antique, cream-colored laid paper from a book, 06.141.

Lindsay Row, Chelsea (w19), 1888. Lithograph printed in black ink on antique, cream-colored laid paper, 06.143.

Chelsea Shops (w20), 1888. Lithograph printed in black ink on antique, cream-colored laid paper from a book, 06.145.

Drury Lane Rags (w21), 1888. Lithograph printed in black ink on antique, cream-colored laid paper, 06.147.

Chelsea Rags (w22), 1888. Lithograph printed in black ink on antique, cream-colored laid paper from a book, 06.148.

The Farriers (w24), 1888. Lithograph printed in black ink on antique, cream-colored japan paper, 06.150. Signed in pencil with the butterfly.

Gants de Suède (w26), 1890. Lithograph printed in black ink on antique, cream-colored laid paper from a book, 06.151.

The Little Nude Model, Reading (w29), 1890. Lithograph printed in black ink on cream-colored laid paper, 06.153.

The Dancing Girl (w30), 1890. Lithograph printed in black ink on cream-colored japan paper, 06.154.

The Horoscope (w32), 1890. Lithograph printed in black ink on off-white wove paper laid down on plate paper, 06.156. Signed in pencil with the butterfly.

Gatti's (w34), 1890. Lithograph printed in black ink on cream-colored japan paper, 06.158.

Hotel Colbert, Windows (w35), 1891. Lithograph printed in black ink on antique, cream-colored laid paper from a book, 06.159.

Cocks and Hens, Hotel Colbert (w36), 1891. Lithograph printed in black ink on antique, cream-colored laid paper from a book, 06.160.

The Garden (w38), 1891. Lithograph printed in black ink on antique, cream-colored laid paper from a book, 06.161.

Lithographs purchased in August 1894

This list corresponds to the one Whistler sent Freer in letter 17, dated 8 August 1894.

1. "The Novel—draped figure." *The Novel. Girl Reading* (w33), 1890. Lithograph printed in black ink on antique, cream-colored laid paper, 06.157. Signed in pencil with the butterfly. Inscribed by Whistler, verso, "(1)."

2. "The seated figure." *The Draped Figure—Seated* (w46), 1893. Lithograph printed in black ink on antique, cream-colored laid paper from a book, 94.13. Signed in pencil with the butterfly. Inscribed by Whistler, verso, "(2)."

3. "Draped figure, back view." *The Draped Figure, Back View* (w67), 1894. Lithograph printed in black ink on antique, cream-colored laid paper from a book, 06.181. Signed in pencil with the butterfly. Inscribed by Whistler, verso, "(3)."

4. "Nude figure—lying down." *Nude Model Reclining* (w47), 1893. Lithograph printed in black ink on antique, cream-colored laid paper, 06.163. Signed in pencil with the butterfly. Inscribed by Whistler, verso, "(4)."

5. "The long Balcony (Paris windows during Carnots funeral)." *The Long Balcony* (w49), 1894. Lithograph printed in black ink on heavy, cream-colored japan paper, 06.165. Signed in pencil with the butterfly. Inscribed by Whistler, verso, "(5)."

6. *The Little Balcony* (w50), 1894. Lithograph printed in black ink on heavy, cream-colored japan paper, 06.166. Signed in pencil with the butterfly. Inscribed by Whistler, verso, "(6)."

7. "The Tête a tête, Garden." *Tête-à-tête in the Garden* (w54), 1894. Lithograph printed in black ink on heavy, cream-colored japan paper, 06.170. Signed in pencil with the butterfly. Inscribed by Whistler, verso, "(7)."

8. *The Long Gallery, Louvre* (w52), 1894. Lithograph printed in black ink on antique, cream-colored laid paper, 06.168. Signed in pencil with the butterfly. Inscribed by Whistler, verso, "(8)."

9. *The Terrace, Luxembourg* (w55), 1894. Lithograph printed in black ink on antique, cream-colored laid paper, 06.171. Signed in pencil with the butterfly. Inscribed by Whistler, verso, "(9)."

10. "The Draped figure, leaning." *Little Draped Figure—Leaning* (w51), 1894. Lithograph printed in black ink on heavy, cream-colored japan

paper, 06.167. Signed in pencil with the butterfly. Inscribed by Whistler, verso, "(10)."

11. "Le Rétameur de l'Impasse." *The Whitesmiths, Impasse des Carmélites* (w53), 1894. Lithograph printed in black ink on heavy, cream-colored japan paper, 06.169. Signed in pencil with the butterfly. Inscribed by Whistler, verso, "(11)." Stamped with Freer's collector's mark.

Lithographs purchased in November 1894
This list corresponds to the one Whistler sent Freer in letter 20, dated 16–17 November 1894.

1. *The Laundress—La Blanchisseuse de la Place Dauphine* (w58), 1894. Lithograph printed in black ink on antique, cream-colored laid paper from a book, 06.174. Signed in pencil with the butterfly. Inscribed, verso, "1."

2. "'The Lady sleeps.'" *La Belle Dame Endormie* (w69), 1894. Lithograph printed in black ink on antique, cream-colored laid paper, 06.183. Signed in pencil with the butterfly. Inscribed, verso, "2."

3. "La belle dame paresseuse." *La Belle Dame, Paresseuse* (w62), 1894. Lithograph printed in black ink on antique, cream-colored laid paper from a book, 06.179. Signed in pencil with the butterfly. Inscribed, verso, "3."

4. "The new draped figure." *Figure Study* (w76), [1894]. Lithograph printed in black ink on antique, cream-colored laid paper from a book, 06.188. Signed in pencil with the butterfly. Inscribed, verso, "4."

5. "Confidences dans le jardin." *Confidences in the Garden* (w60), 1894. Lithograph printed in black ink on cream-colored japan paper, 06.177. Signed in pencil with the butterfly. Inscribed, verso, "5."

6. "The president [?] Dr Whistler." *The Doctor* (w78), [1894]. Lithograph printed in black ink on antique, cream-colored laid paper from a book, 06.190. Signed in pencil with the butterfly. Inscribed, verso, "6."

7. Undetermined.

8. *The Little Café au Bois* (w56), 1894. Lithograph printed in black ink on cream-colored japan paper, 06.172. Signed in pencil with the butterfly. Inscribed, verso, "8."

9. "Les Bébés du Luxembourg." *Nursemaids. "Les Bonnes du Luxembourg"* (w48), 1894. Lithograph printed in black ink on antique, cream-colored laid paper from a book, 06.164. Signed in pencil with the butterfly. Inscribed, verso, "9."

10. "The Smith of the passage." *The Forge. Passage du Dragon* (w72a), 1894. Lithograph printed in black ink on antique, cream-colored laid paper from a book, 06.186. Signed in pencil with the butterfly. Inscribed by Whistler, verso, "for CLF trial or 1st state," and in another hand, "10."

11. "The Forge of the passage du Dragon." *The Smith. Passage du Dragon* (w73), 1894. Lithograph printed in black ink on antique, cream-colored laid paper from a book, 06.187. Signed in pencil with the butterfly. Inscribed by Whistler, verso, "for CLF trial," and by Freer, "Compare with 73a should the latter turn up," and in another hand, "11."

12. "Le robe rouge." *La Robe Rouge* (w68), 1894. Lithograph printed in black ink on antique, cream-colored laid paper, 06.182. Signed in pencil with the butterfly. Inscribed, verso, "12."

13. *The Sisters* (w71), 1894. Lithograph printed in black ink on antique, cream-colored laid paper from a book, 06.185. Signed in pencil with the butterfly. Inscribed, verso, "13."

14. *La Fruitière de la Rue de Grenelle* (w70), 1894. Lithograph printed in black ink on antique, cream-colored laid paper from a book, 06.184. Signed in pencil with the butterfly. Inscribed, verso, "14."

15. "Le Rue de Furstenburg." *Rue Furstenburg* (w59), 1894. Lithograph printed in black ink on antique, cream-colored laid paper from a book, 06.175. Signed in pencil with the butterfly. Inscribed, verso, "15."

16. *La Belle Jardinière* (w63), 1894. Lithograph printed in black ink on antique, cream-colored laid paper from a book, 06.180. Signed in pencil with the butterfly. Inscribed, verso, "16."

17. "La jolie New Yorkaise, Louis Quinze." *La Jolie New Yorkaise* (w61), 1894. Lithograph printed in black ink on antique, cream-colored laid paper, 06.178. Signed in pencil with the butterfly. Inscribed, verso, "17."

18. *Late Picquet* (w57), 1894. Lithograph printed in black ink on antique, cream-colored laid paper, 06.173. Signed in pencil with the butterfly. Inscribed, verso, "18."

19. "The porch." *The Garden Porch* (w140), 1894. Lithograph printed in black ink on antique, cream-colored laid paper, 06.198. Signed in pencil with the butterfly. Inscribed by Freer, verso, "The Garden Porch / Mr. Whistler called it 'The Porch,'" and in another hand, "19."

20. "New draped figure back view (with chair)." *Study* (w77), [1894]. Lithograph printed in black ink on antique, cream-colored laid paper from a book, 06.189. Signed in pencil with the butterfly. Inscribed, verso, "20."

Lithographs purchased in November 1896

This list corresponds to the one Whistler provided in letter 27, dated 28 November 1896.

1. *The Little Steps, Lyme Regis* (w94), 1895. Lithograph printed in black ink on cream-colored laid paper, 96.70. Signed in pencil with the butterfly.

2. *The Manager's Window, Gaiety Theatre* (w114), 1896. Lithograph printed in black ink on antique, cream-colored laid paper, 96.76. Signed in pencil with the butterfly. Inscribed by Whistler, verso, "No. 2."

3. "The Lyme Regis fair." *The Fair* (w92), 1895. Lithograph printed in black ink on cream-colored laid paper, 06.191. Inscribed by Whistler, verso, "No. 3."

4. *Sunday—Lyme Regis* (w96), 1895. Lithograph printed in black ink on antique, cream-colored laid paper from a book, 96.37. Signed in pencil with the butterfly. Inscribed by Whistler, verso, "No. 4."

5. *The Priest's House—Rouen* (w74), 1894. Lithograph printed in black ink on cream-colored laid paper, 96.60. Signed in pencil with the butterfly.

6. "The Brothers—Lyme Regis." *The Brothers* (w91), 1895. Lithograph printed in black ink on antique, cream-colored laid paper, 96.69. Signed in pencil with the butterfly. Inscribed by Whistler, verso, "No. 6."

7. *Mother and Child. No. 2* (w102), [1896]. Lithograph printed in black ink on antique, cream-colored laid paper, 96.72. Inscribed by Whistler, verso, "No. 7."

8. "The Master Smith—Lyme Regis." *The Master Smith* (w84), 1895. Lithograph printed in black ink on cream-colored laid paper, 96.64. Signed in pencil with the butterfly. Inscribed by Whistler, verso, "No. 8."

9. "Little Dorothy." *Little Evelyn* (w110), 1896. Lithograph printed in black ink on antique, cream-colored laid paper, 96.38. Signed in pencil with the butterfly. Inscribed by Whistler, verso, "No. 9."

10. *Girl with Bowl* (w82), 1895. Lithograph printed in black ink on antique, cream-colored laid paper, 96.62. Signed in pencil with the butterfly. Inscribed by Whistler, verso, "No. 10."

11. "The Bonfire—5th November Lyme Regis." *Fifth of November* (w97), 1895. Lithograph printed in black ink on antique, cream-colored laid paper from a book, 06.192. Signed in pencil with the butterfly. Inscribed by Whistler, verso, "No. 11."

12. "The Good Shoe—Lyme Regis." *The Good Shoe* (w86), 1895. Lithograph printed in black ink on cream-colored laid paper, 96.65. Signed in pencil with the butterfly. Inscribed by Whistler, verso, "No. 12."

13. "Fire light, Joseph Pennell." *Firelight. Joseph Pennell. No. 2* (W105), 1896. Lithograph printed in black ink on antique, cream-colored laid paper, 96.74. Signed in pencil with the butterfly. Inscribed by Whistler, verso, "No. 13."

14. "Fire light, Joseph Pennell." *Firelight. Joseph Pennell. No. 1* (W104), 1896. Lithograph printed in black ink on antique, cream-colored laid paper, 96.73. Signed in pencil with the butterfly. Inscribed by Whistler, verso, "No. 14."

15. "Mephisto Smith—Lyme Regis." *The Blacksmith* (W90), 1895. Lithograph printed in black ink on cream-colored laid paper, 96.68. Signed in pencil with the butterfly. Inscribed by Whistler, verso, "No. 16," and by Freer, "Finished State." (Whistler evidently reversed nos. 15 and 16.)

16. *Mother and Child. No. 1* (W80), 1895. Lithograph printed in black ink on antique, cream-colored laid paper from a book, 96.61. Signed in pencil with the butterfly. Inscribed by Whistler, verso, "No. 15."

17. *The Russian Schube* (W112), 1896. Lithograph printed in black ink on antique, cream-colored laid paper, 96.75. Signed in pencil with the butterfly. Inscribed by Whistler, verso, "No. 17."

18. "The Old Smiths Story—Lyme Regis." *The Old Smith's Story* (W98), 1896. Lithograph printed in black ink on antique, cream-colored laid paper, 96.71. Inscribed by Whistler, verso, "No. 18."

19. "The Strong Arm, Lyme Regis." *The Strong Arm* (W89), 1895. Lithograph printed in black ink on antique, cream-colored laid paper, 96.67. Signed in pencil with the butterfly. Inscribed by Whistler, verso, "No. 19."

20. "London, from Savoy—St. Pauls." *Little London* (W121), 1896. Lithograph printed in black ink on cream-colored laid paper, 96.79. Signed in pencil with the butterfly. Inscribed by Whistler, verso, "No. 20."

21. "Waterloo bridge from Savoy." *Waterloo Bridge* (W123), 1896. Lithograph printed in black ink on cream-colored laid paper, 96.80. Signed in pencil with the butterfly. Inscribed by Whistler, verso, "No. 21."

22. "The new Model." *Little London Model* (W130), 1896. Lithograph printed in black ink on antique, cream-colored wove paper from a book, 06.196. Signed in pencil with the butterfly. Inscribed by Whistler, verso, "No. 22."

23. "Charing Cross bridge, from Savoy." *Charing Cross Railway Bridge* (W120), 1896. Lithograph printed in black ink on flecked, cream-colored laid paper, 96.78. Signed in pencil with the butterfly. Inscribed by Whistler, verso, "No. 23."

24. "Little Waterloo—Evening." *Evening. Little Waterloo Bridge* (w119), 1896. Lithograph printed in black ink on flecked, cream-colored laid paper, 96.77. Signed in pencil with the butterfly. Inscribed by Whistler, verso, "No. 24."

25. *The Little Doorway, Lyme Regis* (w83), 1895. Lithograph printed in black ink on cream-colored laid paper, 96.63. Signed in pencil with the butterfly. Inscribed by Whistler, verso, "No. 25."

26. *The Little Steps, Lyme Regis* (w94), 1895. Unidentified. This may have been an additional impression of the lithograph listed above as no. 1, which is no longer in the collection.

27. "The Smiths Yard—Lyme Regis." *The Smith's Yard* (w88), 1895. Lithograph printed in black ink on antique, cream-colored laid paper, 96.66. Signed in pencil with the butterfly. Inscribed by Whistler, verso, "No. 27."

28. "The Butchers dog—Soho." *The Butcher's Dog* (w128), 1896. Lithograph printed in black ink on cream-colored laid paper from a book, 96.81. Signed in pencil with the butterfly. Inscribed by Whistler, verso, "No. 28," and by Freer, "The Butchers Dog—Early state."

Prints purchased in 1900 and 1902

The prints listed below appear in Rosalind Philip's account (letter 66, dated 12 June 1902) and Freer's amended account (letter 67, dated [16] June 1902). The Company of the Butterfly sent the lithographs to Freer through W. S. Marchant on 18 October 1900; Freer received the etchings in August 1899 (see Freer to the Company of the Butterfly, 19 January 1900, FGA Letterpress Book 5).

Father and Son (w87), 1895. Lithograph printed in black ink on antique, cream-colored laid paper, 02.122. Inscribed by Freer, verso, "Purchased from the Society of the Butterfly in March 1900."

Study of a Horse (w95), 1895. Lithograph printed in black ink on cream-colored laid paper, 02.123. Inscribed by Freer, verso, "Purchased from the Society of the Butterfly May 1900."

Needlework (w113), 1896. Lithograph printed in black ink on antique, cream-colored laid paper, 02.124. Signed in pencil with the butterfly. Inscribed by Freer, verso, "From the Society of the Butterfly."

Savoy Pigeons (w118), 1896. Lithograph printed in black ink on cream-colored laid paper, 02.125. Inscribed by Freer, verso, "From the Society of the Butterfly."

Bead-Stringers (K198), 1879–80. Etching, fourth state, printed in brown ink on tan laid paper, 02.120. Inscribed by Freer, verso, "Trial before The butterfly—From Mr Whistler June / 02."

Garden (K210), 1879–80. Etching, seventh state, printed in brown ink on tan laid paper, 02.121. Inscribed by Freer, verso, "From Mr. Whistler—June 1902."

"The Terrace Luxembourg." *Balustrade, Luxembourg Gardens* (K427), 1892–93. Etching printed in brown ink on cream-colored japan paper, 06.123. Inscribed by Freer, verso, "The Terrace Luxembourg."

Café Luxembourg (K434), 1892–93. Etching printed in black ink on tan laid paper, 02.119. Inscribed by Freer, verso, "Cafe Luxembourg."

SELECT BIBLIOGRAPHY

Curry, David Park. "Charles Lang Freer and American Art." *Apollo* 118 (August 1983): 169–79.

————. *James McNeill Whistler at the Freer Gallery of Art.* Washington, D.C.: Freer Gallery of Art, 1984.

Hobbs, Susan. "Whistler at the Freer Gallery of Art," *Antiques* 120 (November 1981): 1194–1202.

Kennedy, Edward G. *The Etched Work of Whistler.* New York: The Grolier Club, 1910. Reprint, San Francisco: Alan Wofsy Fine Arts, 1978.

Lawton, Thomas, and Linda Merrill. *Freer: A Legacy of Art.* Washington, D.C.: Freer Gallery of Art in association with Harry N. Abrams, 1993.

Levy, Mervyn. *Whistler Lithographs: A Catalogue Raisonné.* London: Jupiter Books, 1975.

Lochnan, Katharine A. *The Etchings of James McNeill Whistler.* New Haven: Yale University Press, 1984.

MacDonald, Margaret F. *James McNeill Whistler: Drawings, Pastels and Watercolours, A Catalogue Raisonné.* New Haven and London: Yale University Press, 1995.

Mansfield, Howard. "Charles Lang Freer." *Parnassus* 7, no. 5 (October 1935): 16–18, 31.

Meyer, Agnes E. *Charles Lang Freer and His Gallery.* Washington, D.C.: Freer Gallery of Art, 1970.

————. "The Charles L. Freer Collection," *Arts* 12 (August 1927): 65–82.

Pennell, Elizabeth R., and Joseph Pennell. *The Life of James McNeill Whistler.* 2 vols. Philadelphia: Lippincott, 1908.

————. *The Whistler Journal.* Philadelphia: Lippincott, 1921.

Thorp, Nigel, ed. *Whistler on Art: Selected Letters and Writings of James McNeill Whistler.* Washington, D.C.: Smithsonian Institution Press, 1994.

Tomlinson, Helen Nebeker. "Charles Lang Freer: Pioneer Collector of Oriental Art." Ph.D. diss., Case Western Reserve University, Cleveland, 1979.

Way, T. R. *Mr. Whistler's Lithographs: The Catalogue.* 2d ed. London: George Bell & Sons, and New York: Wunderlich & Co., 1905.

Young, Andrew McLaren, Margaret MacDonald, Robin Spencer, and Hamish Miles. *The Paintings of James McNeill Whistler.* 2 vols. New Haven: Yale University Press, 1980.

Index of Works by
James McNeill Whistler

Paintings are identified by the number (YMSM) given in Andrew McLaren Young, Margaret F. MacDonald, Robin Spencer, and Hamish Miles, *The Paintings of James McNeill Whistler*, 2 vols. (New Haven: Yale University Press, 1980).

Pastels, drawings, and watercolors are identified by the number (M) given in Margaret F. MacDonald, *James McNeill Whistler: Drawings, Pastels and Watercolours, A Catalogue Raisonné* (New Haven and London: Yale University Press, 1995).

Etchings are identified by the title and number (K) given in Edward G. Kennedy, *The Etched Work of Whistler* (New York: The Grolier Club, 1910; reprint, New York: Alan Wofsy Fine Arts, 1978).

Lithographs are identified by the title and number (W) given in T. R. Way, *Mr. Whistler's Lithographs: The Catalogue*, 2d ed. (London: George Bell & Sons, and New York: Wunderlich & Co., 1905).

The "Adam and Eve," Old Chelsea (K175), 138
Annie Haden (K62), fig. 36, 134, 138
Arrangement in Black: La Dame au brodequin jaune—Portrait of Lady Archibald Campbell (YMSM242), 91n
Arrangement in Black and Brown: The Fur Jacket (YMSM181), 89
Arrangement in Black and Gold: Comte Robert de Montesquiou-Fezensac (YMSM398), 177n, 180. See also Count Robert de Montesquiou, No. 2 (W138)
Arrangement in Brown and Black: Portrait of Miss Rosa Corder (YMSM203), 180–81, 185n
Arrangement in Grey and Black: Portrait of the Artist's Mother (YMSM101), fig. 3; purchase by the French government, 16, 79, 82, 83
Arrangement in Grey and Black, No. 2: Portrait of Thomas Carlyle (YMSM137), fig. 35, 16, 21, 131n
Arthur Haden (K61), 138

"The Balcony." See Variations in Flesh Colour and Green: The Balcony
Balcony, Amsterdam (K405), 67, 73n, 138, 200
Balustrade, Luxembourg Gardens (K427), fig. 34, 128n, 165n, 208
Bead-Stringers (K198), 162, 164, 208
Becquet (K52), 138
La Belle Dame, Paresseuse (W62), 99, 203
La Belle Dame Endormie (W69), fig. 4, 100n, 203
La Belle Jardinière (W63), fig. 24, 99, 204
The Blacksmith (W90), 109, 206
Blue and Gold—The Rose Azalea (M1392), plate 8, 102n, 103n,

108n, 112n, 137, 185n
"Blue and Gold Girl." See Harmony in Blue and Gold: The Little Blue Girl
Blue and Silver—Trouville (YMSM66), 43n
The Blue Dress (M468), 95n
"The Blue Girl." See Harmony in Blue and Gold: The Little Blue Girl
Bohemians, Corsica (K442), fig. 38
Bridge, Amsterdam (K409), 67, 200
The Brothers (W91), 109, 205
Brown and Gold (YMSM440), 129n
The Butcher's Dog (W128), 110, 207
By the Balcony (W124), fig. 30

Café Luxembourg (K434), 128n, 164, 208
Cameo, No. 1 (K347), fig. 20, 78, 138
Carlyle, portrait of. See Arrangement in Grey and Black, No. 2: Portrait of Thomas Carlyle
Chancellerie, Loches (K383), 138
Chapel Doorway, Montresor (K395), 138
Charing Cross Railway Bridge (W120), 110, 206
Château Amboise (K393), 138
Chelsea Children (M1511), plate 13, 129n, 162, 164
The Chelsea Girl (YMSM314), 85n
Chelsea Rags (W22), fig. 21, 80n, 201
Chelsea Shops (W20), 201
Churchyard (W17), 201
"La Cigale." See Rose and Brown: La Cigale
Clock-Tower, Amboise (K394), 138
Cocks and Hens, Hotel Colbert (W36), 201
Confidences in the Garden (W60), fig. 6, 25, 99, 100n, 203
Count Robert de Montesquiou, No.

2 (w138), fig. 45, 177n
Courtyard, Rue P. L. Courier
(k368), 138

The Dancing Girl (w30), 201
Dipping the Sail (k325), 138
The Doctor (w78), 99, 203
Dordrecht (k242), fig. 44
The Draped Figure, Back View
(w67), 96, 202
The Draped Figure—Seated (w46),
96, 202
Drouet (k55), 138
Drury Lane Rags (w21), 201
The Dyer (k219), 138

The Embroidered Curtain (k410),
plate 7, 68, 69, 70n, 71, 72,
138
Entrance Gate (w16), 201
Evening. Little Waterloo Bridge
(w119), 110, 207

The Fair (w92), 109, 205
The Farriers (w24), 88n, 201
Father and Son (w87), 162, 164,
207
Fifth of November (w97), 109, 205
Figure Study (w76), 99, 203
Firelight. Joseph Pennell. No. 1
(w104), 109, 206
Firelight. Joseph Pennell. No. 2
(w105), 109, 206
The Forge. Passage du Dragon
(w72a), 99, 204
From Agnes Sorel's Walk (k385), 138
La Fruitière de la Rue de Grenelle
(w70), 99, 204

Gaiety Stage Door (w10), 200
Gants de Suède (w26), 201
Garden (k210), 162, 164, 208
The Garden (w38), fig. 19, 88n, 202
The Garden Porch (w140), 100n,
204
Gatti's (w34), 201

Girl with Bowl (w82), 109, 205
The Good Shoe (w86), 109, 205
The Green Cap (m1527), fig. 42,
165nn
*Grey and Gold: High Tide at
Pourville* (ymsm523), fig. 33
Grey and Silver: The Mersey (m913),
88n
Grey and Silver: Pourville
(ymsm522), 163n, 165n
"Grey and Silver, Trouville." *See
Grey and Silver: Pourville*

*Harmony in Blue and Gold: The
Little Blue Girl* (ymsm421),
plate 2, 27, 40, 112n, 117–18;
and Beatrix Whistler, 21, 22,
113, 116–17; commission for,
19, 87, 92, 94; Freer inquires
after, 107, 115, 128, 148; payment for, 29, 101, 102, 123,
164, 165n
*Harmony in Blue and Gold: The
Peacock Room* (ymsm178), 30,
42
*Harmony in Blue and Silver:
Trouville* (ymsm64), 152n
Harmony in Blue and Violet
(m1076), plate 6, 66n, 69n,
88n, 95n, 137
*Harmony in Brown and Gold: Old
Chelsea Church* (ymsm440),
fig. 11
Harmony in Red: Lamplight
(ymsm253), 40
The Horoscope (w32), 201
Hotel Colbert, Windows (w35), 201
Hôtel de Ville, Loches (k384), 138
Hôtel Lallement, Bourges (k399),
fig. 37, 138

La Jolie New Yorkaise, (w61), 99,
204

"The Lace Curtain." *See The
Embroidered Curtain*

Late Picquet (W57), 99, 204
The Laundress—La Blanchisseuse de
    la Place Dauphine (W58), 99,
    203
Limehouse (W4), 81, 83n
Lindsay Row, Chelsea (W19), 201
The Little Balcony (W50), 96, 202
"The Little Blue Girl." See
    Harmony in Blue and Gold:
    The Little Blue Girl
The Little Café au Bois (W56), 99,
    203
Little Court, Cloth Fair (W18), 201
The Little Doorway, Lyme Regis
    (W83), 110, 207
Little Draped Figure—Leaning
    (W51), 96, 202
Little Drawbridge, Amsterdam
    (K412), fig. 17, 67, 200
Little Evelyn (W110), 109, 205
"Little Lady of Soho." See Rose and
    Gold: The Little Lady Sophie
    of Soho
Little London (W121), fig. 27, 110n,
    206
Little London Model (W130), 109,
    206
The Little Nude Model, Reading
    (W29), 201
The Little Red Glove (YMSM468),
    164, 165n
The Little Steps, Lyme Regis (W94),
    109, 110, 205, 207
Little Venice (K183), 65, 138
The Long Balcony (W49), 96, 202
The Long Gallery, Louvre (W52),
    fig. 25, 96, 202
Long House—Dyer's—Amsterdam
    (K406), 67, 138, 199

Mairie, Loches (K382), 138
The Manager's Window, Gaiety
    Theatre (W114), 109, 205
The Master Smith (W84), 109, 205
Maunder's Fish-shop, Chelsea
    (W28), 77n

The Mill (K413), 67, 69, 70n, 138,
    200
Mother and Child. No. 1 (W80),
    109, 206
Mother and Child. No. 2 (W102),
    109, 205
Mother of Pearl and Silver: The
    Andalusian (YMSM378), 156n

Needlework (W113), fig. 41, 162, 164,
    207
Nocturne (W5), 81
Nocturne: Blue and Gold—
    Valparaiso (YMSM76), 43n, 89
Nocturne: Blue and Silver—
    Battersea Reach (YMSM119),
    plate 16, 156nn, 157, 181
Nocturne: Blue and Silver—Bognor
    (YMSM100), plate 3, 24, 27,
    126n, 132, 133, 136
Nocturne: Dance-House (K408), fig.
    16, 67, 70n, 138, 200
Nocturne: Grey and Silver
    (YMSM156), 95n
Nocturne: Grey and Silver—Chelsea
    Embankment, Winter
    (YMSM205), fig. 47, 181, 185n
Nocturne: Palaces (K202), 138
Nocturne in Black and Gold:
    Entrance to Southampton
    Water (YMSM179), plate 10,
    112n, 115n, 118, 119–20, 120; for
    exhibition in Paris, 133n,
    133–34
The Novel. Girl Reading (W33), 96,
    202
Nude Model Reclining (W47), 96,
    202
Nursemaids. "Les Bonnes du
    Luxembourg" (W48), 99, 203

Old Battersea Bridge (W12), 88n, 201
The Old Smith's Story (W98), 109,
    206
"The Peacock Room" (YMSM178),
    30, 42

"Phryne." See Purple and Gold:
  Phryne the Superb!—Builder
  of Temples
Pierrot (K407), 67, 199
Portrait of Charles Lang Freer
  (YMSM550), plate 5, 31, 158n,
  159n, 160n, 164, 185
Portrait of George W. Vanderbilt
  (YMSM481), 160n
Portrait of Richard A. Canfield
  (YMSM547), fig. 12
The Priest's House—Rouen (W74),
  109, 205
La Princesse du pays de la porcelaine
  (YMSM50), 43n
Purple and Gold: Phryne the
  Superb!—Builder of Temples
  (YMSM490), fig. 9, 28, 129n,
  148n, 162, 164, 165nn
The Purple Cap (M1287), fig. 43,
  165n

Railway-Station, Vovés (K371), 138
Reading (W13), 201
La Robe Rouge (W68), 99, 204
Rose and Brown: La Cigale
  (YMSM495), plate 11; exhibited
  in Philadelphia, 185n; for
  exhibition in Paris, 133, 136,
  162; Freer's purchase of, 123,
  124, 128n, 132, 164
Rose and Gold: The Little Lady
  Sophie of Soho (YMSM504),
  plate 12; exhibited in Munich,
  145, 148; exhibited in
  Philadelphia, 185n; for exhibi-
  tion in Paris, 136, 140; Freer's
  acquisition of, 123, 124, 126,
  127, 130, 132, 133, 162, 164
Rose and Red: The Little Pink Cap
  (M1277), plate 9, 102n, 103n,
  108n, 112n, 137, 185n
Rose and Silver: Portrait of Mrs.
  Whibley (M1415), plate 15, 150,
  152n, 153n, 154n, 154, 156
Rue Furstenburg (W59), 99, 204

The Russian Schube (W112), 109,
  206

Savoy Pigeons (W118), 162, 164, 207
"Self-portrait." See Brown and Gold
The Siesta (W122), fig. 5
The Sisters (W71), 99, 204
The Six Projects (YMSM82–87), 29,
  38
Sleeping (M1293), 165n
The Smith. Passage du Dragon
  (W73), fig. 26, 99, 204
The Smith's Yard (W88), 110, 207
Square House, Amsterdam (K404),
  67, 200
Steps, Amsterdam (K403), fig. 1, 67,
  138, 200
The Strong Arm (W89), 109, 206
Study (W77), 99, 204
Study of a Horse (W95), 162, 164,
  207
Sunday—Lyme Regis (W96), 109,
  205

The Terrace, Luxembourg (W55),
  96, 202. See also Balustrade,
  Luxembourg Gardens
Tête-à-tête in the Garden (W54), 96,
  202
The Thames in Ice (YMSM36), plate
  14, 40, 45n, 150–51, 153n, 154n,
  154, 156
Tour St. Antoine, Loches (K392), 138
The Tyresmith (W27), 77n

Under the Cathedral, Blois (K397),
  138

Variations in Flesh Colour and
  Green: The Balcony (YMSM56),
  plate 1, fig. 23, 94, 132; engraving after, 90; exhibited at
  Society of American Artists,
  18, 88; exhibited at World's
  Columbian Exposition, 18–19,
  89, 91n; Goupil exhibition,

17; Memorial Exhibition in Boston, 40; purchase by Cavafy, 17; purchase by Freer, 18, 88; published in *Harper's*, 18, 88; sale to Kennedy, 18, 151, 152n
Venice (M802), 95n
Venus Rising from the Sea (YMSM93), 11
Victoria Club (W11), 200
Violet and Silver: The Great Sea (YMSM298), 186n
"The Violet Cap." *See The Purple Cap*
A Violet Note—Spring (M1395), plate 4, 25, 115, 137, 147; Freer's purchase of, 102n, 103n, 108n

Waterloo Bridge (W123), 109, 206
Weary (K92), 138
"Whistler's Mother." *See Arrangement in Grey and Black: Portrait of the Artist's Mother*
The Whitesmiths, Impasse des Carmélites (W53), 96, 203
The White Symphony: Three Girls (YMSM87), fig. 10, 29–30, 38
Windsor (Memorial) (K329), 138
The Winged Hat (W25), 77n
Writing on the Wall (M1396), fig. 40, 148n, 165n, 129n

Zaandam (K416), 67, 199

General Index

Alexander, John White, 181, 186n
American Car and Foundry
  Company, 23
Amsterdam etchings. *See under*
  etchings
Anglo-Boer War, 31, 160n
Ashbee, C. R., 158n
Avery, Samuel P., 42n

Bancroft, J. C., 18
*The Baronet & the Butterfly. See
  Eden versus Whistler*
Bell, Nancy (Mrs. Arthur), 34, 45n,
  177n
Bell, William, 71, 78
Bernheim, George, 151, 152n
Bixby, William K., 156n, 163n, 164
Boldini, Giovanni, *Whistler Asleep,*
  fig. 32
Boston. *See* Memorial Exhibition
Boussod, Valadon & Cie., Paris,
  81, 85n
Buffalo. *See* Pan-American
  Exposition
Bunkyō, Matsuki, 189

Canfield, Richard, 35, 177; and the
  Society of American Artists,
  35, 180, 184, 188
Carter, Walter S., 72, 73n
Cassatt, Alexander J., 85n
Cavafy, G. J., 17–18

Cavafy, John, 18, 152n
Chapman, Alfred, 24, 126n
Champs de Mars. *See* Société
  Nationale des Beaux-Arts
Chase, William Merritt, 186n, 196;
  Sargent's portrait of, 181, 186n
Chelsea Old Church, 31, 37
Chicago. *See* World's Columbian
  Exposition
Church, Frederick Stuart, 74, 196;
  The Fog, 75n.
Company of the Butterfly, 28–29;
  123, 125n, 208; etchings from,
  91n, 127, 128n, 151; accounts
  with, 161–62, 164–65
Copley Society, Boston, 39–40
Cowan, John James, 26, 150–51,
  153, 154
Cox, Kenyon, 182–83, 186n

Detroit Free Press, 15, 65, 194–98
Dewing, Thomas Wilmer: and
  Freer's patronage, 18; in Paris,
  20, 43n, 97, 101, 106; Whistler
  on, 103
Doherr, Captain, 105–7
Dunthorne, Robert, 141
Duret, Théodore, 80n

Eden, Sir William, 24, 125n
*Eden versus Whistler. The Baronet
  and the Butterfly* (Whistler),
  24–25, 44n, 123–24

Etchings (Whistler): exhibition of, 89, 134, 137–38, 140, 141; Amsterdam, 14–15, 65, 67–68, 70n, 72, 76; Corsica, 141; Paris, 91n; Venice, 82, 84, 87, 90. *See also under* Company of the Butterfly; Hecker, Frank J.

Exposition Universelle (1900), Paris, 25, 129n, 156n

Fine Art Society, London, 77n, 197

Franklin, Maud, 37

Freer, Charles Lang, plate 5, fig. 2, fig. 39, 12; and Asian art, 20, 37, 41; and Asian travels, 21, 94, 104–7; business career of, 14, 23; in Capri, 128, 137, 143, 185; commissions Whistler, 19, 87, 92, 94; and duty on art, 81, 104, 127, 140, 155; illness of, 130, 132; meets Whistler, 13–14, 65, 93, 194–98; as patron, 18, 27; print collection of, 13–15, 19, 67, 76, 82, 90, 94; on Whistler, 14, 37, 39, 86; Whistler collection of, 24, 27, 29–30, 38, 39–41; and Whistler's illness and death, 32–33, 36–37, 46n; on Whistler's late works, 23–24, 28. *See also under* lithographs; *Portrait of Charles Lang Freer;* Whistler, Beatrix

Freer, Emma Frances, 146–47, 148n

Freer, George Townsend, 169n, 176n

Freer, Watson, 83n, 84

Freer Gallery of Art, Washington, D.C.: Asian art in, 41–42; first-floor plan, fig. 15; and Freer's bequest, 9, 40–41; as tribute to Whistler, 13, 42, 44n; Whistler's letters in, 10

Gardner, Isabella Stewart, 134, 135n

The Gentle Art of Making Enemies (Whistler), fig. 18, 70, 75n, 110n

Glasgow: Corporation of, 16; University of, 9

Glasgow Herald, 85n

Godwin, E. W., 66n, 77n

Goupil Gallery: in London, 16, 83n, 135n, 152n; in New York, 188n; in Paris, 135n, 140, 141; "Nocturnes, Marines, & Chevalet Pieces" (1892 exhibition), 16–17, 84, 88n, poster for, fig. 22; *Nocturnes—Marines—Chevalet Pieces* (photographs), 90, 91n. *See also* Marchant, W. S.

Grolier Club, New York, 42n, 65, 68, 91n

Haden, Francis Seymour, 134

Hagenbeck, Karl, 105–06

Harper's, 18, 88

Havemeyer, Henry O., 42n

Havemeyer, Louisine, 22, 37

Hecker, Anna (Mrs. Watson Freer), 80, 82, 84

Hecker, Frank J., 20, 69n, 75n, 104; etchings for, 67, 69–70; lithographs for, 79, 82, 83, 92, 94, 95, 100n, 109–10, 111

Heinemann, William, 21, 34, 110n, 123, 175; and *The Gentle Art,* 70n, 75n

Helleu, Paul Cesar, *Portrait of Whistler,* fig. 13.

Hessele, Charles, 152n

Hiffernan, Joanna, 37

Hitchcock, J. Ripley, 70n

Hunterian Art Gallery, Glasgow, 9

International Society of Sculptors, Painters, & Gravers, London, Second Exhibition (1899), 125n, 126n, 128n

Jerome, Thomas Spencer, 144n
Johnson, John G., 94

Kennedy, Edward Guthrie, 18, 23,
   90, 151, 156n; catalogue of
   etchings, 91n, 139n. *See also*
   Wunderlich & Co.
Kingsley, Elbridge, 98n
Knoedler, M., New York, 188

La Farge, John, 184
Leyland, Frances (Mrs. Frederick
   R.), portrait of, 95n
Lithographs (Whistler): 15, 79, 83,
   87, 90, 92, 104, 111, 112n;
   accounts for, 95–96, 99–101,
   109; color, 79, 82, 87; exhibi-
   tion of, 134, 148; final, 21, 22;
   Freer on, 23, 94; Freer's col-
   lection of, 76, 77n, 81–82. *See
   also under* Hecker, Frank J.
London. *See* Fine Art Society;
   Goupil Gallery; Grosvenor
   Gallery; International Society
   of Sculptors, Painters, &
   Gravers
Low, Will H., 180–84, 185n
Luxembourg, Musée du, Paris, 16,
   80

MacMonnies, Frederick William,
   20–21, 43–44n, 97, 108;
   Triumph of Columbia, 97
Mallarmé, Stéphane, 80n
Mansfield, Howard, 13, 73n, 103,
   134, 156n; and Amsterdam
   etchings, 14, 65, 68, 76
Marchant, W. S., 127, 131n, 151, 154,
   155, 156n, 208
Melchers, Gari, 148n
Memorial Exhibition (1904),
   Boston, fig. 14, 39–40, 46
Menpes, Mortimer, photogravure
   of Whistler by, frontispiece, 25
Meyer, Agnes, 13, 22, 42, 43n

Montesquiou, Robert de, portraits
   of, 177n, 178n, 180
Montross Gallery, New York, 27,
   139n
Moore, Augustus, 75
Morris, Harrison S., 34–35, 181,
   186n
Munich, VIII Internationale Kunst-
   Austellung (1901), 145, 147–48

National Art Association, 86
New York. *See* Grolier Club;
   Knoedler; Montross Gallery;
   Society of American Artists;
   Wunderlich & Co.
"Nocturnes, Marines, & Chevalet
   Pieces." *See under* Goupil
   Gallery
*Nocturnes—Marines—Chevalet
   Pieces. See under* Goupil
   Gallery
Notes (Whistler lithographs), 76, 81
"'Notes'—'Harmonies'—
   'Nocturnes'" (1889 exhibition),
   New York, 88n

Orchar, J. G., 181

Palmer, Emma W., 39
Pamington, Lillie, 165n
Pan-American Exposition (1901),
   Buffalo, 136
Paris. *See* Boussod, Valadon, &
   Cie.; Exposition Universelle;
   Goupil Gallery; Luxembourg,
   Musée du; Société Nationale
   des Beaux-Arts
Pennell, Elizabeth R.: on Freer, 37;
   and Whistler, 31–32, 34; as
   Whistler's biographer, with
   Joseph Pennell, 8–9, 31, 36
Pennsylvania Academy of the
   Fine Arts exhibition (1903),
   Philadelphia, 34–35, 181–82
Philip, Ethel. *See* Whibley, Ethel
   Philip

Philip, Frances Black, 66n, 122n
Philip, John Birnie, 66n
Philip, Rosalind Birnie, fig. 7, fig.
    41, 33, 37, 122n, 150, 158n,
    161n, 168; correspondence
    with Freer, 9, 150–51, 153, 161,
    171, 174–75, 191; gift to
    Glasgow, 9; in The Hague,
    33, 167n, 171, 174; and the
    Pennells, 8; as Whistler's
    executor, 33, 37–38, 39
Plumb, R. E., 21–22, 111
Prellwitz, Henry, 186n

Rawlinson, William George, 155,
    157, 181
Robertson, W. Graham, 185n
Roosevelt, Theodore, 40; Sargent's
    portrait of, 35, 182
Ruskin, John, 83n

Salon, Paris, 102n
Sargent, John Singer: *Portrait of
    Theodore Roosevelt,* 35, 182;
    William Merritt Chase, N.A.,
    181, 186n; works exhibited in
    Munich, 148n
Seligman, André J., 177n
Smithsonian Institution, 40–41
Société Nationale des Beaux-Arts,
    Paris, 102n, 135n, 142n, 165n
Society of American Artists, New
    York: 1892 exhibition, 18, 88,
    91; 1903 exhibition, 35–36,
    180–85, 187–88
Stevens, G. N., 185n

Thayer, Abbott Handerson:
    A Virgin, 19; *Stevenson
    Memorial,* 186n
Theobald, Henry Studdy, 26–27,
    29, 44n, 161n
Thomson, David Croal, 16, 151
Tryon, Dwight William, 98n

Vanderbilt, George W., 160

Way, T. R., *Portrait of Whistler,*
    fig. 28, 30, 77n, 83n
Way, Thomas, 76, 77n
Wedmore, Frederick, *Whistler's
    Etchings,* 139n
West Point, 124, 125n
Whibley, Ethel Philip, plate 15, fig.
    6, 25, 33, 150, 152n, 153, 154,
    156, 172n, 174
The Whirlwind, 75–76
Whistler, Beatrix, figs. 4–6, fig. 24,
    fig. 30; correspondence with
    Freer, 9, 69–70, 72, 74, 79,
    81–82, 83–84, 86–87, 105–7;
    friendship with Freer, 15, 21,
    65, 103, 105–06, 113–14; illness
    and death of, 21–22, 107,
    110n, 114; marriage to
    Whistler, 66n. *See also under
    Harmony in Blue and Gold:
    The Little Blue Girl*
Whistler, James McNeill, fron-
    tispiece, fig. 8, fig. 13, fig. 28,
    fig. 32; affection for Freer, 22,
    113; and America, 19; and
    Asian art, 20; biography of,
    8–9, 39; in Corsica, 25, 27,
    133–35, 136, 141, 143; and
    English appreciation, 16–17,
    24, 26, 83–84, 123, 157; frame
    by, 65; and Freer's collection,
    24, 28, 123, 145, 151; gifts to
    Freer, 24–25; in The Hague,
    32–33, 167–76; on himself, 24,
    142; illness and death of,
    32–33, 36–37, 121, 126, 130, 133,
    141, 174, 193n; marries Beatrix,
    66n; on patronage, 23, 26–27,
    42; in Pourville-sur-Mer, 24,
    121–22; proposes Paris exhibi-
    tion in 1901, 133–34, 136–37,
    143–44, 145
Whistler, John, 85n
Whistler, William, 85n
Whittemore, J. Harris, 156n
Witenagemote Club, Detroit, 15, 65

Wolf, Henry: engraving after
    *Portrait of Richard A.
    Canfield,* fig. 12; engraving
    after *Portrait of Thomas
    Carlyle,* fig. 35.
World's Columbian Exposition
    (1893), Chicago, 18–19, 84, 86,
    89–90, 97n
Wunderlich & Co., New York:
    and etchings, 69; Freer's pur-
    chases from, 17, 23, 77n, 87,
    88n, 95n, 114, 139; exhibitions,
    87, 100n. *See also* Kennedy,
    Edward Guthrie